"The American colonists will fight back," Benjamin Franklin warned the King of England. **"They are not as easily frightened as you believe they will be."**

But the king and many in Parliament thought this was hilarious. These ragtag Americans didn't even have an organized army. And they would attempt to stand up to the British, the greatest military power on earth? Absurd! King George was certain that the presence of British soldiers and warships would strike fear in the hearts of the colonists. Then, like children, they would calm down and behave.

It didn't turr

A Background Note about *A Nation Created: The War for American Independence*

Because the American Revolution took place more than 230 years ago, it is sometimes thought of as a rather dull and distant event that no one can relate to anymore. After all, life in the 1700s was very different from the world we know today. Men wore powdered wigs, and women were expected to wear heavy skirts that reached the floor. Roads were dirt; transportation was by horse; and entertainment usually came in the form of plays or books. And when it came to warfare, the greatest weapons available were clunky cannons and muskets that could accurately fire a bullet only 50 yards. How exciting could a war from this era be?

Pretty exciting, actually.

Everyone loves an underdog, and when the American colonists took on England, the world's greatest military power in 1776, people worldwide began rooting for this brave little upstart country of America. Weaving through the story of the Revolution was a mighty cast of colorful characters. Spies, snipers, and even a guerrilla leader known as "the Swamp Fox," filled the dark woods of the original thirteen colonies. The eccentric and brilliant Benjamin Franklin won over the French people with his wit and his beaver-fur hat. And a tiny sea captain named John Paul Jones fought in blood up to his ankles, refusing to give up the fight.

Pulling all of this together was the remarkable spirit of the American people. With little more than a small, untrained army, brave leaders, and a determination to win independence from British rule, Americans headed into a war that would ultimately end in one of the biggest upsets in military history.

A NATION CREATED

The War for American Independence

MARK THOMAS

TP THE TOWNSEND LIBRARY

A NATION CREATED:
The War for American Independence

TP **THE TOWNSEND LIBRARY**

For more titles in the Townsend Library,
visit our website: **www.townsendpress.com**

Townsend Press, Inc.
439 Kelley Drive
West Berlin, NJ 08091
permissions@townsendpress.com

ISBN-13: 978-1-59194-245-0
ISBN-10: 1-59194-245-4

Library of Congress Control Number:
2011928356

CONTENTS

CONTENTS

CHAPTER 1

"America must fear you"

*O*n a warm October morning in 1781, a strange sight appeared at the top of a hill in Yorktown, Virginia. In the haze of smoke from cannons and gunfire, a small soldier in a bright red coat was walking directly toward the enemy.

"It's the British!" shouted an American soldier. "They're preparing a surprise attack from that far hill!"

But as the soldier drew closer, the Americans could see that he was only a young boy. He walked alone, playing a continuous drumroll, and he stood straight, perhaps in an attempt to look brave and tall. The boy was too far away for the Americans to see the tears of terror that streaked his dusty face. Finally, the boy stopped, barely fifty yards from the Americans. Perhaps a hundred muskets were pointed at him. He looked straight ahead, his thin legs shaking uncontrollably. But his drumming never stopped.

"Hold your fire!" came the command from an officer who knew what this continuous drumroll meant.

"Don't shoot!" the soldiers shouted to one another, eyeing the drummer curiously. What could this mean?

Sometimes drummer boys tapped a sharp, quick drumbeat that meant it was time to attack. Sometimes a different kind of irregular rhythm meant to turn around and run away from the battle. But this uninterrupted drumroll sent out a very rare kind of message. It was one the Americans had not heard once before during six long years of fighting.

An unusual silence fell over the battleground as the soldiers listened and watched. For nearly five minutes, the only sounds were the wind blowing in from the Chesapeake Bay and the constant drumming. Then another British soldier, a grown man, slowly appeared behind the boy. His shoulders drooped, and he frowned sadly. But he held both of his hands high over his head to show that he carried no weapons. And in his right hand he waved a white piece of cloth back and forth.

Surrender!

"Huzzah! Huzzah!" came the excited cheer from the Americans. Was it really possible? Had the mighty British military finally been brought to its knees? As soldiers celebrated, shouts of "It's a miracle!" mingled with the cheers. It was, truly, very difficult for many of these American men to believe that they had beaten such a strong enemy, such a giant.

If it was difficult for the Americans to believe, it was nearly impossible for the British to comprehend. Many refused to accept that this shameful and embarrassing loss could really have happened. Two days after waving the flag of surrender, thousands of British soldiers marched out into a wide field, surrounded by rows and rows of American soldiers. It was the tradition in the 1700s for the losing side's soldiers to throw their weapons into a huge pile to show that they were no longer a threat.

"They looked like angry schoolboys who had just received a whipping," one American remembered. "Mostly they looked like they wondered how an army like ours had ever beaten an army like theirs."

As the pile of British guns grew, the British military band struck up a tune. Usually during a surrender ceremony like this, the losing side showed respect by playing songs that celebrated the winners. But not today. Instead, the British band loudly played a popular song called "The World Turned Upside Down."

• • •

If ponies rode men and if grass ate cows,
And cats should be chased into holes by the
mouse,
If summers were spring and the other way
around,
Then all the world would be upside down.

The intended message was clear. The British soldiers would not even look at the victorious Americans, and the British army's general was so upset that he had pretended to be too sick to attend the surrender ceremony. Some British soldiers claimed that he stayed in his tent all day crying. This all went beyond being sore losers; the British really felt that nothing was as it should be. Truly, the world had turned upside down.

How had this happened? The story of this miraculous victory is the story of a war in which unbelievable odds were beaten and in which, even in the worst of circumstances, brave men and women refused to give up believing either in themselves or in their dream of freedom. It is the story of the American Revolution. But while this story ended with a loud cheer, it had begun quietly enough.

Thirteen colonies stretched out along the Atlantic Ocean. They made up what was known simply as "America" in the 1700s. There was no

"United States" yet, because there were no states—only areas that were colonies, or possessions, of England. And these colonies were hardly what anyone would describe as "united." Most people living in the colonies had never traveled more than ten miles away from their homes. Roads were so few and so bad that it took two weeks just to get a letter from Boston to Philadelphia! As a result, the people of the original thirteen colonies knew very little about one another. A man from Virginia, for example, may never even have met a man from New York, and if he had, he had probably eyed him with suspicion.

"They seem in a hurry to go everywhere," a Virginian wrote of New Yorkers in 1745 when he visited their colony. "They dress most oddly, and though we speak the same language, they are exceedingly difficult to understand!"

Truly, in the early 1700s, the thirteen colonies were more like thirteen separate countries than like the one country we now know as America. There was, however, a common bond—a common thread of interest—among all the colonists: England. Most colonists had originally come from England and continued to think of it as their "mother country." They wore clothes made of British cloth, drank British tea, followed British politics, and waited impatiently for newspapers and books to make their way across the Atlantic Ocean on ships from England. Colonists living in South Carolina might not have a clue about what life was like in neighboring North Carolina, but they knew even the smallest details of recent trends and scandals in London.

And colonists did not call England the mother country simply out of affection and love for their country of origin. England, like a parent, protected the young colonies and provided them with many of the things they needed to "grow up" and become strong. Although the British king and his government (called "Parliament") encouraged the colonies to provide for themselves, finding the appropriate place to draw the line between protection and independence often proved challenging. The king worried that if the colonies became too independent, they would not need England anymore. And the colonies were full of rich resources and possibilities—which the king certainly did not want to lose.

Living on the edge of a new and unsettled country was often frightening. There were strange wild animals, dark unexplored forests, and, perhaps most fearsome of all to the colonists, Indians. These Native Americans were the original settlers of the land, and they had lived there for many thousands of years. Their culture was quite advanced, with organized settlements and inventive farming methods. But many of the colonists viewed them only as dangerous half-dressed savages who spoke a bizarre language and fought brutally when their land was threatened. Some colonists even believed that the natives were evil spirits and devils in human form.

If it was unsettling for colonists to know that Native Americans lived nearby, it had been downright terrifying when, in 1754, the natives had joined the French in a war against the colonists. Although France already owned a sizable chunk of North America, it had wanted even more land. For many years, French traders and fur trappers who lived in Canada had dealt peacefully with Native Americans, generally treating them with respect and fairness. The French had easily convinced the natives to join them in their fight against the colonists. In return, the French promised to leave the Native Americans alone and not take over their lands.

The British did not want France interfering with their colonies. Eventually, the king and Parliament decided it was time to drive the French out of America altogether. What followed was nine years of fighting known as "the French and Indian War." Although many American colonists (including a twenty-five-year-old George Washington) fought in that war, England provided thousands of British soldiers and nearly all the weapons and supplies the colonists needed.

By 1763, the war was over, and the British had led America to victory.

Americans were extremely grateful to the British. Songs of praise were written for the new king of England, George III. The colonists sent many gifts to England by ship. Young boys played "war" dressed in the bright red coats of the British soldiers, and young girls perfected the art of serving British tea. What, then, could have so interfered with this love and harmony to lead to a war with England barely ten years later? Two things: money and power.

By the end of the French and Indian war, England had racked up a debt that would be equal to about $4 billion today. Making matters worse, England had the expense of supporting more than 10,000 British soldiers who remained in America to protect the colonies. In addition, the jobs that the war had provided in England were gone. Homeless families soon filled the streets of London, and people began rioting and demanding that the government do something to fix the economy. The leader of Parliament, the prime minister, came up with a simple solution.

"We have run ourselves into an immense debt to give the Americans protection," the prime minister, George Grenville, announced. "And now they must contribute a small share toward the expense."

In other words, he wanted to start taxing the colonists. He suggested placing a tax on a large list of paper goods, including such items as legal documents, books, newspapers, and even playing cards and calendars. Colonists would be required to buy stamps in the amount of the tax, and then place the stamps on these paper goods before they could legally use them. This would be called "the Stamp Act."

Some members of Parliament thought this was a very bad idea. For many generations, Americans had repaid England through loyalty and hard work to settle a new territory for the mother country. Being forced to pay a tax on top of this might make colonists angry. After all, Britain owned this new country. It wasn't the colonists' fault if this ownership was creating debt.

But the new king dismissed these warnings as though he was fanning away annoying gnats. He thought taxation sounded like a wonderful idea. King George was barely 22, and he had neither the patience nor the experience to consider the backlash that might result from taxing people who lived 3,000 miles away. In addition, the governors of each colony had been appointed by King George (as opposed to being elected by the colonists), so enforcing the tax would be no problem, right?

"And everyone who does not agree with me is a traitor and a tyrant," King George concluded flatly, as he ordered the Stamp Act to go into effect in the spring of 1765.

Perhaps King George's biggest mistake was that he did not understand Americans at all. He had never visited America, mainly because he saw no reason to do so. The King believed that the colonists were really not much different from British people. Perhaps the Americans were a little less stylish and cultured, but, like his British subjects, they would obviously do as they were told. King George was certain that they would not dare to disobey their king.

However, the young king was wrong.

"No taxation without representation!"

When they learned about the new tax, colonists from Charleston to Boston took to the streets, angrily shouting this slogan. Essentially, the colonists were saying, "We did not have a voice in this decision! You can't just slap a tax on us without our input!"

For more than 150 years, the colonists had been making their own decisions. Even though the colonies belonged to England, the people in America had generally governed themselves. Granted, England stepped in to protect its investment now and then, but for the most part, the British government had allowed the colonists to make their own laws and create their own taxes. Now, Americans were angry with King George about this crazy Stamp Act. It would take more than shouting in the streets to get rid of the tax, however.

In Boston, a writer and political activist named Samuel Adams came up with a simple solution. The stamps had to be distributed by an official agent. What if there were no agents to hand out the stamps and collect the money? Then the tax would die before it even began. Adams encouraged the people of Boston, and beyond, to threaten the stamp agents and, hopefully, scare them away from their assignments.

What greater joy did New England see
Than a stamp man hanging on a tree?

This brief poem was attached to a life-sized doll hanging by a noose from an elm tree in Boston. This display made Boston's stamp agent, Andrew Oliver, a bit nervous, but he was not particularly frightened. Much later that evening, however, the doll's head was cut off, and its body was set on fire. An angry mob then marched to Oliver's house and hurled the doll's head through Oliver's front window. Andrew Oliver quickly decided to quit his very short-lived career as a stamp agent.

Throughout the colonies, groups that called themselves "the Sons of Liberty" threatened and harassed stamp agents. Soon, just as Samuel Adams had hoped, there was no one left to distribute stamps and collect money. Back in England, King George sulked and argued, but he finally had to admit that the tax was not going to work. When the Stamp Act was canceled, the colonists celebrated their victory and once again returned to cheering and supporting their beloved king and the wonderful British people. New Yorkers were so grateful to King George that they built a huge statue of him and placed it in the middle of the city.

But King George wasn't feeling the same love for his disobedient colonists.

"It is our right to tax them!" he pointed out to his favorite adviser, Frederick North, who would later become prime minister. "They are behaving exactly like spoiled children."

So, within the year, Parliament approved new taxes on many items, such as paper, glass, paint, wine, and tea, that were shipped from England to America. This time there were no stamps involved, just an amount of money to be collected. Perhaps King George had thought the colonists would not be as offended by what seemed more like a simple price increase than a tax, but the Americans were not so easily fooled.

Immediately, colonists refused to buy any of the British goods. As much as Americans loved British tea, many of them instead began drinking what they considered a rather dull and unpopular drink: coffee.

The protest went well beyond the boycott, however. Things turned violent when tax collectors (the men assigned to collect the taxes from merchants) were chased down and beaten with clubs. Some tax collectors who refused to stop working received the particularly gruesome punishment of tarring and feathering. First they were stripped naked and covered in hot tar. Then they were rolled in goose feathers and paraded around town.

"The worst of it was trying to get the tar off," one tax man later wrote. "Whole chunks of skin came off with the dried tar."

Meanwhile, tempers flared at American ports where British guards and tax agents watched for smugglers who were attempting to sneak in goods from other European countries without paying taxes on them. One of these smugglers was a rich Boston merchant named John Hancock. Like his friend Sam Adams, Hancock believed that the new taxes were terribly unfair, and he was more than willing to do his part to fight this injustice by bringing in a shipload of tax-free wine. When British soldiers seized his ship full of wine, Hancock was furious. A large gathering of the Sons of Liberty stood on the docks with their fists clenched and their anger building as they watched Hancock argue with the British guards.

"If you are men, behave like men!" Sam Adams finally shouted to those gathered. "Let us take up arms immediately and be free!"

Finally, it had come to this. Americans were now beyond protest and were ready to fight back with guns if necessary. In London, King George huffed around and again complained to his adviser, Frederick North. When the king wondered out loud if these new taxes should be canceled too, North strongly objected. In North's opinion, it was time to teach these disrespectful Americans a lesson. He thought it would be better to send over more British soldiers than to give in again.

"America must fear you," North explained to the young king, "before she can love you."

CHAPTER 2

"The town of Boston ought to be destroyed!"

*O*f course, no one likes to pay unfair taxes, and American colonists were no exception. But the anger and frustration that the colonists felt went far beyond the issue of money. Many Americans felt that both the British king and many British people were beginning to look down on them. The British seemed to think of Americans as lower-class, as rowdy loudmouths who needed the firm guidance of the wiser and greatly superior British.

During this time in England, people were rigidly separated by class. Those who had a lot of money and came from important families were given endless respect and opportunities, regardless of how unintelligent or lazy they might be. Meanwhile, the poor and those who came from powerless families remained powerless. They had no say in the way things were done in

England. Therefore, the worst taxes and the most unfair treatment always plagued the lower classes and ordinary people. Now, Americans began to feel as though they, as a group, were being treated the same way.

Colonists did not like such treatment—especially colonists in Massachusetts, who had been governing themselves for nearly 150 years. They had set up their own government, had elected officials to make decisions for the entire colony, and had written their own code of laws. In short, they had learned that ordinary people can govern themselves.

Today, this may seem like an obvious and unremarkable statement, but in the mid-1700s, it was a groundbreaking and somewhat dangerous idea. Nowhere in the world were leaders simply "ordinary." They were kings and queens. They came from long lines of wealth and privilege. They had been born into their positions of power. The idea that an everyday person could earn respect and gain power through hard work was unthinkable. And the idea that middle-class and lower-class people could have a hand in making decisions was considered a joke.

Across the Atlantic Ocean in London, sixty-year-old Benjamin Franklin thought about this new idea of ordinary people governing themselves. Franklin was an American, but he had moved to London as a representative of the colonies and also, Franklin had to admit, because he found life in London to be a lot more exciting than life back home. Franklin loved parties and theater and flirting with beautiful women. He loved culture and conversation and big cities. But now, the attitudes of the British were beginning to annoy and worry Franklin.

It didn't matter that Franklin was a brilliant inventor who had discovered electricity and had invented bifocals, the Franklin stove, and even swim fins. Although he was famous worldwide for his writing and wit, those abilities did not earn him much respect in political circles in London. After all, Franklin's father had been nothing more than a candle maker. And Franklin, though admired and accomplished, did not come from money or royalty. Perhaps he amused some members of Parliament, but no one took him very seriously. So now, as King George and Frederick North plotted and planned to send warships to Boston Harbor, Franklin's protests were ignored.

"The American colonists will fight back," Franklin warned. "They are not as easily frightened as you believe they will be."

But the king and many in Parliament thought this was hilarious. These ragtag Americans didn't even have an organized army. And they would attempt to stand up to the British, the greatest military power on earth? Absurd! King George was certain that the presence of British soldiers and warships would strike fear in the hearts of the colonists. Then, like children, they would calm down and behave.

It didn't turn out quite that way.

"Hey, bloody-back!" "Go back home, you filthy lobster-backs!"

The Sons of Liberty and many other residents of Boston gathered along the streets to shout taunts and insults at the arriving British soldiers. Because the soldiers wore bright red wool coats as part of their uniforms, they were often called names having to do with blood or lobsters. This may not seem like the worst of insults, but it was upsetting to the British, who were unusually proud of their fancy uniforms.

In reality, the British military outfit was rather ridiculous, and the colonists wasted no time in pointing this out. The heavy red coats were covered with brass buttons, emblems, and a lot of frilly lace. The collar of the coat was made of stiff leather so that the soldiers were forced to stand unnaturally straight and were barely able to turn their heads. Many of the "Redcoats," as the British soldiers were called, wore very heavy brass helmets that had to be shined every morning. Beneath his helmet, each soldier was required to wear his hair in a tight ponytail with one wide (but not too wide!) curl above each ear. This rule was strictly enforced; men who had not properly powdered and greased their hair were often punished. Completing the uniform were bright white knee britches that were so tight that they had to be put on wet. As they dried, they became so snug that they sometimes cut off circulation.

Although these were not the most comfortable uniforms to wear, British soldiers believed that the uniforms brought them respect. They didn't receive much respect, however, as they paraded through Boston and set up their tents in Boston Common. Young boys followed behind the Redcoats, laughing and pointing. Men shouted, and threw garbage and stones at them. As time passed, townsmen began picking fistfights and getting into brawls with soldiers. In many ways, this was unfair to the British soldiers. Most of them were seventeen- and eighteen-year-old boys from poor families; being a soldier was the only job they could get. They hated being in Boston every bit as much as the Bostonians hated having them there.

For two years, tension built. Samuel Adams and Sons of Liberty groups began pushing for armed attacks on the soldiers in order to force them to leave.

"Why are they even here?" Adams asked angrily. By that time, many of the Redcoats had moved their tents onto the property of Boston residents, who, naturally, did not welcome them. "It is our right as colonists to defend our property," Adams pointed out. Still, no shots were fired—until a cold night in March of 1770.

It's strange to think that an argument over a wig started what would come to be known as "the Boston Massacre." Although it seems amusing to think of today, wigs were very popular among men in the 1700s. In particular, British army officers loved their white powdered wigs with fancy curls. And on this particular night, a British officer had apparently left a wig shop without paying.

"Stop him! Stop that damned bloody-back!" shouted a young apprentice wigmaker named Edward Garrick. "He's stolen that wig!" Garrick ran through the snow after a British officer, who finally stopped and shouted back that he *had* paid for the wig. Out from the shadows came one of the officer's soldiers, who, to defend his leader's honor, walked over to Garrick and whacked him on the head with the butt of his rifle.

Gradually, a crowd gathered. Insults were shouted back and forth between angry townspeople and a growing group of British soldiers. As the crowd pressed closer to the soldiers, some of the Redcoats raised their guns.

"You wouldn't dare fire at us!" the mob

yelled and taunted.

"Stand back!" the British warned again and again.

The crowd then began throwing snowballs—some filled with rocks and oyster shells—at the soldiers. Moving to the front of the mob was a tall black man named Crispus Attucks. Attucks had escaped from slavery twenty years earlier, and he was not afraid to confront these soldiers, who had been sent from England to limit the freedoms of Americans. Later reports claimed that Attucks had a large club in his hand. At the moment he raised it, a shout was heard from the back of the gathered soldiers:

"Fire!"

Suddenly, the soldiers began shooting into the crowd. The first to fall—the very first man to die in what would become known as "the American Revolution"—was Crispus Attucks. Six more men were shot, and four of them later died of their injuries. Five deaths do not normally make a "massacre," but colonists were stunned and furious. They wanted a name for this event that would be remembered, a name that sounded as horrible as this event had seemed to them.

Bostonians insisted that all the British soldiers involved in the Boston Massacre be tried and executed. But who would defend the soldiers in a trial? Everyone assumed that no lawyer in his right mind would stand up for the Redcoats. However, John Adams, a well-known lawyer from Massachusetts and cousin of Samuel Adams, accepted the case. In court, Adams argued that the soldiers had fired only in self-defense.

"Place yourself in the situation of the soldiers," Adams said. "The crowd is crying, 'Kill them! Kill them!' They are heaving snowballs, clubs, and sticks three and a half inches in diameter. Consider yourselves in this situation, and then judge. . . ."

In the end, all of the soldiers were found "not guilty." Many Boston citizens were, at first, very angry. But over time, when tempers cooled, most people came to see that John Adams had done the right thing. He had shown that, by defending even one's enemy in the name of justice, ordinary people *can* govern themselves.

After the Boston Massacre, King George was a bit alarmed. He wanted Americans to obey him and fear him, but he had not wanted bloodshed. In an attempt to cool things down, King George ordered all of the British troops to leave Boston. Some troops returned to England, and others moved north to Canada so that they would be close enough to keep an eye on the hotheaded colonists.

As for the taxes that had started all this

trouble in the first place, the king and Parliament decided to get rid of all taxes on the colonists— except one.

"I am clear that there must always be one tax to keep up the right," King George announced, "and as such, I approve the tea tax."

Colonists were not happy with this remaining tax, but most of them shrugged their shoulders and continued either drinking that dreadful coffee or smuggling in tea from Holland. Meanwhile, entire warehouses of boycotted tea were rotting in London. Americans' refusal to buy British tea was not only insulting; it was damaging England's already-weak economy. As usual, King George turned to Frederick North, who was now prime minister, for advice. North felt that the plan he eventually came up with was brilliant. The colonists, however, felt otherwise.

All of England's tea was imported from colonies in India that were part of the British Empire. England, then, worked as the middleman in distributing tea around the world. Until the boycott, America had been England's biggest customer. North realized that if the tea were shipped directly from India to America, the cost of tea would go way down—so far down that England could keep the tax on it and the tea would still be cheaper than tea that was being smuggled from Holland.

Of course, North could just as easily have removed the tax. Americans would have returned to buying British tea, and all ill feelings between the colonists and the king might have disappeared. But both North and King George were stubborn. They insisted on keeping that one tax to "keep up the right." If they could trick Americans into paying this one tax, they would remain the ones in charge. They—not the colonists—would have the power.

But just as the colonists had not been easily frightened, they were not easily tricked.

"So the king thinks we are fools, does he?" a merchant from Philadelphia asked angrily. "We are not ignorant to his schemes. He merely wants the smuggler gone, and his hated tax around our necks!"

In seaports up and down the coast, huge groups of colonists gathered and shouted, "Resist! Resist!" as they locked arms and blocked the unloading of British tea ships. And in Boston, Sam Adams and his Sons of Liberty group met on a cold December evening in 1773.

"Saltwater tea for us all, boys!" Adams shouted with a wink. "Boston Harbor a teapot tonight."

This was a pre-planned signal, though no one is certain whether it was, in fact, Sam Adams and his "boys" who were responsible for what happened next. Sometime later that night, dozens of colonists disguised as Mohawk Indians walked quietly toward Boston Harbor. War paint streaked their cheeks, and feathers were tied around their heads. They carried tomahawks, hatchets, and swords and moved very quickly along the docks. Then they crept aboard three ships loaded with tea.

It must have been a strange sight—a large group of men in costume splitting open chests full of tea and then dumping the tea overboard into the water of the harbor. What would later become known as "the Boston Tea Party" wasn't really a party at all. The men worked quietly and efficiently, following strict orders to neither take any of the tea nor celebrate with shouts or laughter as they threw tea into the water. In fact, one man who was found stuffing tea into his pockets was punished by being stripped naked and being ordered to walk the three miles back to his house. As the men dumped the tea, they respectfully swept off the decks of the ships and were careful not to damage anything on the ships other than the tea.

Meanwhile, the ships' British crews just stood aside and watched. They were neither angry nor frightened.

"They had no quarrel with us," one colonist explained. "Ours was not a demonstration against those fellows, but against their king and his tax. We had no interest in falling into battle with any of them."

About three hours later, when the colonists were finished dumping the tea, they cleaned off the docks, repaired a door that had been broken on one of the ships, and quietly went home.

It may have been a peaceful-enough demonstration, but when news of the Boston Tea Party spread the next day, many colonists became energized and excited about this clear show of disrespect for King George and his tea tax.

"This is the most magnificent movement of all," John Adams wrote in his diary. "There is a dignity, a majesty in this last effort that I greatly admire."

However, King George and Parliament did not find the Boston Tea Party majestic. In fact, they were very angry about it.

"It was the most unprovoked insult given to civil power in recorded history," one member of Parliament dramatically announced.

More to the point, another member shouted, "The town of Boston ought to be boxed about their ears and destroyed!"

In agreement, the British government decided to punish Boston by passing four new laws that would become known in America as "the Intolerable Acts." The laws were given this name because punishments were so unfair that colonists could not tolerate them. One act moved the capital of Massachusetts from Boston to Salem as a way of humiliating Bostonians. Another act put an end to Massachusetts' colonial government—so highly valued by its citizens—and provided that, instead, King George would make all decisions for the colony. A third act allowed British soldiers to live in and take over any private buildings they wanted in Massachusetts: Schools, homes, and even churches could be turned into barracks.

But the fourth Intolerable Act was the worst: King George ordered Boston Harbor closed until the people of Boston paid for all the tea that had been thrown overboard. Closing the harbor would put thousands of Bostonians out of work. It would shut down the trade and fishing industries. It would, in a short period of time, completely destroy Boston's economy. King George knew all this, but he didn't care.

"The Americans must fear me before they can love me," he reminded himself. Certainly the destruction of Boston would be a terrifying warning to the colonists, King George thought. The other twelve colonies would not dare disrespect their king after such a mighty show of power.

Then, as before, the unexpected happened: Instead of fear, many of the colonists felt only anger at the king and concern for the people of Boston. Loads of fish, meat, grain, rum, cash, and clothing flooded into Boston from the other colonies. King George's plan had backfired in a truly magnificent way. Thirteen separate colonies that had basically ignored one another for 150 years were suddenly pulled together.

In taverns, town halls, churches, and homes—and on street corners all through the colonies—people began gathering and talking. For the first time, urgent news flowed from colony to colony. And for the first time, people began to feel as though they lived in their own country, a country they supported and loved.

In Virginia, a fiery young man named Patrick Henry, who was well known for giving inspiring speeches and for supporting the rebellion against the king, stood up at a large gathering. A hush fell over the crowd as Henry said what was in the hearts of many colonists.

"The distinctions between Virginians, Pennsylvanians, New Yorkers, and New Englanders are no more," Henry said firmly. "I am not a Virginian, but an American!"

CHAPTER 3

"Blows must decide"

*W*ord drifted back to England that Americans were supporting one another by lending a hand to help colonists in Boston, who were suffering under the Intolerable Acts. Rather than worrying about this, many British people found it funny.

"The colonies are like thirteen quarrelsome sisters," one member of Parliament joked. "They will soon be bickering again."

However, King George wanted to make sure that the colonists did not even have the opportunity to meet together. When he found out that Virginia, in particular, was working both to help Bostonians and to unify the colonies, the king shut down the Virginia government. But, as usual, Americans were not so easy to control. Virginia's most important leaders held a secret meeting in a tavern in Williamsburg. There they made emotional speeches and brainstormed plans for helping the colonists in Boston. One of the speeches was made by one of Virginia's most-respected men, George Washington.

"If need be," the tall, low-voiced Washington announced, "I will raise one thousand men, supply them at my own expense, and march with them, at their head, for the relief of Boston."

But the most important decision to come out of the meetings in the Williamsburg tavern was the decision to form a new group that would be made up of representatives from all of the colonies.

"A Congress should be appointed," the Virginians agreed, "a Congress to plan for the defense and preservation of our common rights."

This "Continental Congress," as it was named, would welcome any leaders from the thirteen colonies who were willing to work hard to figure out how to make peace with England. At this point, Americans were not thinking about war. They were thinking mostly about how King George and Parliament could be persuaded to put an end to their unfair and often harsh treatment of colonists. Most Americans still believed that their king was a reasonable man who had just made some bad decisions.

And so, in September of 1774, fifty-six leaders from twelve colonies (Georgia decided not to participate) gathered in Philadelphia,

Pennsylvania. The group included some of the greatest leaders of the day: Massachusetts lawyer John Adams, the fiery Samuel Adams, George Washington, Benjamin Franklin (who, fed up with England, had returned to America), the wealthy and patriotic John Hancock, and the outspoken Patrick Henry.

While all those gathered agreed on the goal of this First Continental Congress, nearly everyone had a different opinion about how this goal of working things out with England should be achieved. Debates went on for hours, until some people lost their voices. Even the smallest issues raised big disagreements.

"If someone had declared that three plus two equaled five," John Adams later wrote to his wife in frustration, "members would have wasted two days debating the details of that issue!"

But, finally, common ground was found, and decisions were made. It was decided to formally condemn the Intolerable Acts as being illegal. Furthermore, members agreed that as long as British troops occupied Boston, Americans should increase the intensity of their boycott of everything imported from Britain. It was further agreed that no one really wanted to enter into a war with England over these issues.

Across the Atlantic Ocean, however, King George did not feel the same way at all. The king was furious to find out that the colonies had formed their own congress and were making their own decisions about *his* laws. In addition, he began to worry when he saw, as one member of the Congress described it, "thirteen clocks now striking as one."

"The colonies are in a state of rebellion," King George announced. "Blows must decide whether they are to be subject to this country or independent."

When members of the Continental Congress realized that King George had lost his temper and that war was just around the corner, many of them suggested changing the wording of the decisions that had been made. They thought that perhaps a representative should go to England to speak directly with King George. They wanted to do something, *anything*, to keep the peace. But not all members of the Congress agreed.

"Is life so dear, or peace so sweet, as to be purchased at the price of chains and slavery?" Patrick Henry boomed in anger. "Forbid it, Almighty God! I know not what course others may take; but as for me, give me liberty or give me death!"

As it turned out, "the course" that many colonists were taking was much like Henry's. Even though the Continental Congress had focused on how to avoid war, everyone had the prickly sense that war was becoming more and more likely.

"I know not where the sensation began," wrote a minister in Philadelphia. "But thoughts of war that would have made me faint twelve months ago now flutter like wings in my chest! I am not afraid—no, I'm almost exhilarated!"

In every corner of the colonies and in every town and city, men gathered to plan for the defense of their homes. Stockpiles of weapons and ammunition were gathered, and small bands of soldiers, called "militias," were formed. In addition, there came to be a new kind of soldier, known as a "minuteman." Most minutemen were young, physically fit men who, when called upon, could be armed and ready to fight within a minute of being warned that the enemy was approaching. Colonists knew that the only chance their small local militias would have against the British forces would lie in the element of surprise.

Although many Americans may have been excited about the idea of war, many British people were not.

"This war would be unnatural, unconstitutional, unnecessary, unjust, dangerous, hazardous, and unprofitable," London's *Evening Post* complained.

More to the point, another London paper

referred to King George as a "foolish, obstinate, and unrelenting King."

Most of the British troops shipped to Boston to control the colonists were not happy to be there. Although they understood *why* they were in America, they had no enthusiasm for fighting this looming war. Like the British crews who had stood by as colonists tossed tea into Boston Harbor, many soldiers felt that the "war" was between the Americans and King George— not between the Americans and the British. At the same time, however, British soldiers were growing extremely tired of the daily harassing from the colonists in and around Boston. Many soldiers began looking forward to a battle just as a way of venting their frustrations.

As tensions mounted daily in Boston, the British general Thomas Gage became more and more worried. Gage favored keeping the peace as long as possible, but tempers were becoming so short that he feared there would be another incident like the Boston Massacre. After an argument between a British soldier and a Bostonian ended with the soldier firing his pistol into the air, Gage refused to allow soldiers to carry guns in the streets of Boston.

"Gage is mostly always scared and nervous," one young soldier wrote home to England. "We now all call him 'Old Woman' behind his back."

King George didn't even bother going behind General Gage's back. He continually wrote critical letters to his general, letting him know that the clock was ticking and that if he didn't attack the colonists soon, he would be replaced. In particular, the king wanted Gage to do something about those two loudmouths, Samuel Adams and John Hancock. As the unavoidable war grew closer, Adams and Hancock had been in the forefront of stirring Bostonians into a frenzy of anger against the British. Now the king was impatient. It was time for the British to strike.

Gage sighed as he paced back and forth at his headquarters in Boston. He knew he had to follow his king's orders, but what should he do? It wasn't like the Americans had an army ready and waiting for a battle. And it wasn't like the British could just randomly attack Boston for the sake of an attack. Finally, General Gage came across some secret information that sparked a plan for the first battle of the Revolutionary War.

A great store of weapons and ammunition had been accumulated in an old warehouse in the town of Concord, about seventeen miles west of Boston. And, anticipating that British soldiers would soon be after them, both Adams and Hancock were hiding in the town of Lexington, on the way to Concord. Gage thought, *Why not make a surprise capture of Adams and Hancock and then move on to make a surprise capture of the military supplies?*

The key word was "surprise." And unfortunately for Gage, Boston was full of men and women who spent their days closely watching the British. A loosely formed spy ring surrounded Boston, and while Gage thought his secret was safe, Bostonians knew well in advance that the British were planning an attack somewhere. They watched the soldiers packing and preparing. They noticed that the troops were practicing more drills. And about a week before the attack, a young stable boy, always ignored by the soldiers, overheard a conversation.

"These troublesome colonists will surely be running scared when they see us come through," bragged one soldier to his friend.

"Yes, and it won't be long now," the other agreed. "Not long at all."

The stable boy slipped out of the shadows and ran to the home of one of the organizers of Boston's spy ring. Once the organizer, named Paul Revere, knew that the attack was about to happen, he and his fellow spies could easily guess that the target of the attack would be the weapons stores in Concord, with a very likely stop to grab Adams and Hancock. But when, exactly, would the attack take place? The militias in both Concord and Lexington were placed on high alert. Then there was nothing left for the spies in Boston to do but to wait and watch. As soon as it became obvious that the British were headed to Concord, Revere and a friend named Billy Dawes would rush ahead and warn the townspeople.

But as Revere and his spies waited, there was one more problem to iron out: The city of Boston was practically an island. It was surrounded by the Charles River on all sides with only a very thin strip of land, known as "Boston Neck," leading out of the city. Revere knew that Gage would have soldiers blocking Boston Neck to keep anyone from escaping Boston and warning the colonists. In addition, Revere knew that British warships would be guarding the waters of the Charles River.

What if Revere and Dawes could not get out of Boston to warn people?

Revere came up with a plan: The Old North Church in Boston had a very tall bell tower that could be seen from across the Charles River in a town called Charlestown. Revere knew that the British would sail to Charlestown once they left Boston. Therefore, Revere decided to send a warning across the river by lighting either one or two lanterns in the bell tower on the night the British made their move (and he was sure the troops would leave at night). One lantern would indicate that troops were traveling across land through Boston Neck; two lanterns would mean they were sailing across to Charlestown.

Finally, on the night of April 18, 1775, Revere watched as British soldiers lined up and headed to one of their warships, the *Somerset*. In a flash, Billy Dawes took off on horseback for Boston Neck. As expected, it was heavily guarded, but Dawes knew the area better than the British did, and somehow he sneaked past. Meanwhile, to indicate that the British would be approaching by water, Revere ordered the lighting of two lamps in the Old North Church. Then he crept down to the Charles River, where an old rowboat and two friends were waiting.

A full moon shone down on the Charles, and there was barely a breath of wind. To get across the river, Revere and his friends would have to pass right by the *Somerset*. This would be exceedingly tricky; they would have to be absolutely quiet. The friends began rowing, and . . .

"Stop!" whispered Revere with a panicked look around. The rusted old oarlocks made a grinding and clanking sound every time the oars swung back. "It's too noisy. We need something to muffle it."

The men rowed back to the shore and sat in silence for a moment. Then one of them grinned.

"I think my girlfriend may have what we need," he whispered. Bounding out of the boat, the young man dashed just down the street, stood beneath a window, and whistled. When the woman opened her window, a strange sight followed. The two talked briefly, and then, looking somewhat embarrassed, the young woman slipped off her flannel petticoat and threw it down to her boyfriend.

Oars wrapped in flannel make no noise at all. Revere slipped past the *Somerset* with its sixty-four guns, and he was soon met on the banks of Charlestown by another friend, who held the reins of a very fast horse.

"We saw the lanterns, Paul, and the word is spreading," Revere's friend said breathlessly. "But you must spread it faster!"

Paul Revere leaped onto the horse, took the reins, and disappeared quickly down a dark road. He had to get to Lexington in time to warn Adams and Hancock, but as he flew through the small towns and villages around midnight, he warned everyone else, too.

"The British are coming! The British are coming!" Revere is said to have shouted for miles as he sped through the countryside. (In reality, he probably shouted, "The regulars are coming!" as *regulars* was the word commonly used for British soldiers.)

In the middle of the night, Revere arrived at the house in Lexington where Adams and

Hancock were hiding. He had arrived well ahead of the British, who were way behind schedule. General Gage had miscalculated how many soldiers the *Somerset* could carry, and, as it turned out, the ship had to make two trips to Charlestown instead of one.

Revere begged Hancock and Adams to hurry. However, Hancock had other ideas.

"Bring me my gun! Where's my sword?" Hancock shouted, hurrying around in his pajamas.

"Certainly you're not thinking of fighting," Adams said to his friend in an alarmed voice.

"Certainly I am!" Hancock bellowed.

"But we're politicians, not soldiers," Adams argued back.

Revere sighed and headed to the kitchen for some food, just as his friend Billy Dawes arrived. The two men took a brief break and then continued their ride, shouting warnings all the way to Concord.

Perhaps an hour or more later, Adams had finally convinced Hancock to escape rather than fight. With bundles of belongings slung over their shoulders, the two were still debating and arguing as they hurried down an empty street and then out into an open field. As a cold wind blew across the frosty field, Adams looked back on the quiet town. In nearly every window, candles burned as young men waited, their rifles in hand. The first glimmer of a pink sunrise shone in the east.

"What a glorious morning!" Adams suddenly exclaimed.

Hancock looked at him doubtfully, as though he might debate that point, too.

"I mean," Adams explained, "what a glorious morning for America!"

CHAPTER 4

"Don't fire till you see the whites of their eyes!"

*"I*f you go one inch further, you are a dead man!"

Paul Revere's luck finally ran out on the way to Concord. British patrol soldiers, who had been sent a day earlier to keep an eye out for Revere and his spies, caught up with him about five miles east of Concord. Revere shouted a quick warning to Dawes, who took off on his horse through the thick woods.

The British soldiers pointed their guns at Revere and threatened to kill him, but in the end they simply took his horse and weapons and left him standing in the road as they continued on to Concord. Meanwhile, Dawes, in his tremendous hurry to escape, was knocked off his horse by a tree limb and was, at 3:00 in the morning, wandering aimlessly around the dark woods.

Luckily, a third man, Samuel Prescott, had decided to join Revere and Dawes in Lexington. He had escaped down the road unseen, and now he rushed on to Concord. Though Paul Revere is generally given all the credit for warning the colonists that the British were coming, it was actually a group effort.

Just after dawn on April 19, 1775, the British marched into Lexington. Their leader, Major John Pitcairn, was an energetic officer who was certain that the Americans would give up quickly as soon as they learned what fighting the British was like.

"I am sure that one active campaign, and the burning of two or three of their towns, will set everything right," Pitcairn said confidently. "Nothing but this will ever convince these foolish bad people that England is in earnest."

Usually, Pitcairn was a lively officer who enjoyed joking with his men and keeping everyone's spirits high. But as his soldiers came into Lexington, Pitcairn was not in a particularly good mood. Because of all the delays back in Boston, the British were now hours behind schedule. Pitcairn and his men had been ordered by Gage to continue straight on to Concord and to forget about trying to capture Adams and Hancock (who were now long gone anyway). Pitcairn was obviously hungry for a fight, and he had hoped the first one would come in Lexington. As it turned out, he would get his wish.

"Major, sir!" shouted a soldier. "Look to the town common."

Lined up on the green grass in the center of town were seventy minutemen, their guns in their hands. Their leader, Captain John Parker, was not nearly as eager for bloodshed as Pitcairn was. Now, as the British approached, Parker looked at his minutemen. Some were as young as 16, and some were as old as 50, but all of them looked frightened. Not only were they outnumbered by the British 200 to 70, none of these new soldiers had ever been in a battle.

"Let the troops pass by," Parker ordered quietly. "Don't shoot unless they shoot first."

The British began to pass without incident, but Pitcairn decided he didn't like the sight of Americans holding guns.

"Lay down your arms, you damned rebels!" Pitcairn shouted at the minutemen.

But the minutemen didn't budge.

"Why won't you lay down your arms?" Pitcairn demanded, beginning to lose his temper.

What happened next has remained a bit of a mystery since that morning in 1775. The Americans claimed that someone on the British side fired at them. The British, on the other hand, claimed that the shot came from the American side. In any event, that first gunshot has become known as "the shot heard 'round the world," because it started the first battle of the American Revolution.

The Battle of Lexington lasted barely five minutes. It was a quick frenzy of confusion and shouting, with most of the minutemen running away and most of the British firing on them. When the musket smoke cleared, eight Americans had been killed and nine wounded. On the British side, only one soldier had been slightly injured. Although it hadn't been much of a battle, the British troops fired a "victory volley" and, without a look back, continued on their way to Concord.

Once in Concord, the British found only a few rifles and a small container of bullets in the storehouse where they had expected to find a mountain of weapons. Because they had been warned hours earlier, the residents of Concord had moved all the weapons to dozens of hiding places—in the hills, in private homes, and even in holes dug in the ground. Frustrated and angry, the British troops spread out and searched all over Concord for the hidden weapons. Before long, a second wave of British soldiers had caught up to Pitcairn's regiment, bringing the number of British troops close to 800 men.

About 250 minutemen had been waiting for the British, but when they saw how outnumbered they were, they took to the surrounding hills. Throughout the morning, as the British poked and prodded around Concord, minutemen from all over the countryside gathered in the hills. Soon there were nearly 500 of them. They positioned themselves above the bridge that led out of Concord; they hid behind trees, boulders, and bushes. As soon as the British assembled to leave and began crossing the bridge, called North Bridge, the Americans started shooting. The British soldiers were totally baffled. No one fought like this in Europe! British armies were used to fighting the enemy face to face in long, orderly lines.

"These bloody colonists do not know how to wage a fair and honest fight," one soldier later wrote home bitterly. "It was as if men came down from the clouds!"

And men continued to "come down from the clouds" all the way back to Boston. For seventeen miles, minutemen opened fire from the hills, from behind buildings, and even from treetops. It seemed as though a flood of men had gathered from every imaginable corner of the countryside. By day's end, more than 3,600 men from forty towns had arrived to take shots at the British. At first, the British were ordered to fire back. Then they were instead ordered to march quickly. Finally, they were ordered to run.

British losses on April 19 were high, with 73 men killed and 174 wounded. General Gage was completely stunned. He had never believed that the Americans would fight back so fiercely. Reluctantly, he sent King George a letter with the bad news, ending his letter like this: "If you had thought ten thousand more soldiers was sufficient, send twenty thousand."

Back in Boston, John Adams stood on a hillside that evening, watching the frightened and ragged British soldiers limp back into town. He observed them with mixed feelings. It had not been long ago that Americans had felt a real bond with the British and had proudly considered themselves part of the British Empire.

"When I reflect and consider," Adams wrote later that night, "that the fight was between those whose parents but a few generations ago were brothers, I shudder at the thought."

Adams was not the only one shuddering. There were many Americans, particularly in New York City, who were utterly opposed to fighting the British. Like King George, they felt that the colonists should be grateful for everything the British had done for America. What harm could there be in Americans being asked to pay a few taxes? It didn't seem as though the king was asking for too much.

The Americans who remained loyal to King George and sympathized with the British were called "Loyalists." Those who opposed the king and were willing to fight for freedom from unfair British rule were known as "Patriots." Throughout the war, the tension between Patriots and Loyalists would often be just as fierce as the tension between Patriots and the British. And even by mid-1775, some Loyalists were being chased out of towns, fined huge sums of money, and harassed endlessly.

In the week following the battles of Lexington and Concord, militias from all over New England continued to stream into and around Boston. By the end of April, 20,000 armed Patriots had gathered there. The Americans took over and blocked Boston Neck, and they would not allow British boats to cross the Charles River. British soldiers, therefore, became trapped in Boston. If they were going to go anywhere, it would have to be back out to sea. That was where the Patriots hoped they would go. However, a month later, the British stubbornly remained, trapped but ready to fight.

While the Americans and British continued staring one another down in Boston, a group of Patriots known as "the Green Mountain Boys" received an interesting message from a spy in northern New York: "Fort Ticonderoga is in ill repair, and it is poorly guarded. The British are completely unprepared for an attack."

"Fort Ti," as it was called, was an old French fort on the Hudson River. No one had paid much attention to the fort for about fifteen years. After the French and Indian War, the British had occupied the fort and had used it as a storage place—for a hundred or more cannons. Now, as all-out war crept closer, the Patriots realized that they could make good use of those cannons. The leader of the Green Mountain Boys was Ethan Allen, a six-foot-six-inch giant of a man with a very short temper and a love of fighting. He didn't need to look twice at the message from the spy.

"Boys," he said to his gang, "we're going to Fort Ti."

In the dead of night, Allen and his men charged the fort, hollering and screaming at the top of their lungs. It so terrified the only British guard (who had been sound asleep) that he himself screamed and then ran away. Allen then stood at the bedroom door of the fort's commander and bellowed a lot of insults and threats until the commander shakily opened his door.

Within minutes, Fort Ticonderoga was surrendered to the Patriots. The Green Mountain

Boys cheered and then rushed down to the fort's cellar to look at the cannons—huge iron monsters that weighed several hundred pounds apiece. A few of the men stared at the cannons and scratched their heads. How on earth would they get the cannons from northern New York to Boston? As they stood contemplating this problem, a shout arose from the far side of the cellar.

"Rum! Ninety gallons of rum, boys!"

All worries about hauling cannons suddenly disappeared. Legend has it that Ethan Allen and his Green Mountain Boys partied for three days at Fort Ticonderoga. After a day of recovery, they settled down to the issue of transporting sixty tons of cannons across 300 miles of bad roads.

Meanwhile, an emergency meeting of the Second Continental Congress was called in Philadelphia on May 10. Some members of the Congress were not at all impressed by Ethan Allen's storming of Fort Ticonderoga. Some people still felt that an agreement could be made with King George and that colonists should be working to *avoid* war with Britain, rather than working to encourage it. But many in the Congress, including John Adams, rolled their eyes at the idea of finding common ground with King George at this point. The king had shown them that he had no intention of backing down.

Nonetheless, the members of this emergency meeting of the second Congress wrote a letter begging King George to rethink what he was doing and to remove the British troops from Boston. Even though the letter was urgent, it still took weeks to get to England—and additional weeks for a response to make its way back to America. As members of the Congress waited patiently for the king's reply, impatient Patriots began taking matters into their own hands.

Ships full of British soldiers had continued to come into Boston Harbor. Now there were thousands of troops trapped in the city. The British commanders felt that it was time to break out of this trap. As a first step, the commanders decided to take over two nearby hills that looked out over the camps of American militias. These hills, Bunker Hill and Breed's Hill, were perfectly placed for lobbing cannonballs at the Americans and forcing them to back away from Boston.

This plan was labeled top-secret by the British, but, as with nearly every plan the British made, spies almost instantly figured out what the Redcoats were up to. As a result, on June 16, 1775, twelve hundred Patriots spent the entire night on Breed's Hill, hastily building a fort. In the morning, the British were astounded.

"There, in the morning light," one soldier wrote, "was suddenly a completed fort where, only the evening before, there had been nothing more than trees and wind."

Immediately, the British planned an attack. Row after row of Redcoats began marching up Breed's Hill toward the fort. Colonel William Prescott, who was commanding the American militia, saw three problems as he looked at his men: The men had only fifteen rounds of ammunition apiece; they were terribly scared; and most of them had never been in a battle before. Prescott considered these facts and came up with a plan.

"Don't fire till you see the whites of their eyes!" Prescott shouted, hoping that this would help his frightened shooters to aim accurately and to save their ammunition.

The long battle that followed turned out to be the bloodiest battle of the entire Revolution. The British struggled up the hill, only to be slaughtered by the Americans.

"The Redcoats couldn't keep their footing," one Patriot recalled, "because the blood, so much of it, made the grass like sheer ice."

Yet as one wave of British soldiers fell, another would make its way up the hill. Finally, after three attempts, the British reached the fort and captured it. Before the sun set that day, the British army suffered more than 1,000 casualties (men killed, wounded, captured, or missing). The Americans suffered over 400 such casualties. Although the Americans had run out of ammunition by the end of the battle, many of them continued to fight, using the butts of their guns, rocks, fists, and even their teeth.

"Those people show a spirit and conduct against us that they never showed against the French," claimed an appalled General Gage, who had fought with Americans in the French and Indian War.

After "the Battle of Bunker Hill" (as it was called, even though it was fought on Breed's Hill), there was little doubt in anyone's mind that the Americans and the British were now headed into real war. There would be no reconciling with King George. As if to emphasize this fact, the king's response to the second Congress's letter finally arrived.

"The Americans are wicked and desperate persons," King George had written angrily. "They are in open rebellion, and every attempt should be made to bring the traitors to justice!"

CHAPTER 5

"'Tis time to part"

"*B*ring the traitors to justice."

These words from King George made the members of the Second Continental Congress a little anxious. This was not just some vague threat that the king was throwing around in anger. The "justice" he referred to was a very specific and brutal punishment reserved for those who were traitors to their king and their country. In the mid-1700s treason was considered one of the worst crimes a person could commit, and the astonishingly horrid punishment was made to fit the crime.

First, a traitor was hanged on the gallows until he was almost dead. Then, just when he was about to die, he was cut down and revived a bit. Next, his intestines were cut out and set on fire right in front of him. The traitor was usually dead by this point, but death was guaranteed when, next, his head was chopped off and his body was cut into four pieces. Then, as the final insult, the traitor's remains were placed on spikes and displayed around the city of London.

As members of the second Congress gathered to discuss war plans and preparations, each man knew very well that if the war were not won, this dreaded punishment would be his fate. The members of Congress, or the "Founding Fathers," as they came to be called, were the leaders of this Revolution. If the war were lost, they would be the first ones King George would go after. However, it was not fear of punishment that made the Founding Fathers so determined to win the war—it was fear of America's loss of independence. "Give me liberty, or give me death" was not just a catchy saying; it expressed the Founding Fathers' belief.

All successful armies need great leaders. And getting great leaders was the first order of business for the second Congress in the summer of 1775. Who should be the commander of the new American army? As always, there was a lot of debate, disagreement, and arguing before a decision was reached. Because he had been so outspoken about fighting the British, John Hancock was certain that he would be chosen, even though he had no military experience. In addition, Hancock's close friend John Adams was the member who would ultimately make the final decision.

Although Hancock didn't know it, John Adams had another man in mind—a more modest man, a man with a lot of military experience, and a man who seemed to be a natural commander. When Adams rose to announce his decision, Hancock looked around, smiling proudly, believing he was about to hear his name.

"I have made my choice," Adams said, "and I nominate the gentleman from Virginia—George Washington."

When Hancock heard this announcement, his smile vanished instantly. Somewhat amused, Adams wrote to his wife later that evening: "I never remarked a more sudden and striking change of countenance [facial expression]."

At the same time that Hancock's smile was turning to a frown, George Washington jumped up and ran out of the room. Although this may seem like odd behavior, Washington did not want to be present—even for a minute—while his fellow members of Congress discussed him. Washington wanted every member to feel free to say what he liked or didn't like about Washington. The nomination of Washington was surprising to some. Unlike Hancock or other outspoken leaders, George Washington was a quiet man who was not fond of dramatic speeches and loud opinions. But everyone in Congress knew that Washington was a good man and a strong leader. For once, there was very little debate: George Washington would be the commander.

Today, the image that George Washington's name most often brings to mind is the picture of him on the one-dollar bill: old, white-haired, and frowning. However, in 1775, Washington looked nothing like this. He was a fairly young man at 43, and curly reddish-blond hair covered his head. He was not thought of as particularly handsome, but he had quite a commanding presence. At six feet two and 200 pounds, he towered above most of the men of his day (the average height for a man in the 1700s was five feet five).

Because of his size and his quiet ways, some people referred to Washington as "the quiet giant." However, Washington was not quiet because he had nothing to say. On the contrary, he was often silent so that he could listen to the views of others before expressing his own ideas. And, in many ways, Washington preferred a quiet life. He was happiest at his home and farm in Virginia, caring for his many horses and planting new trees—far from the roar of politics and battles. Like many of the greatest military commanders, Washington was no fan of war.

"My greatest wish," Washington once claimed, "is to see this plague of mankind, war, banished from the earth."

As honored as Washington was to be named commander, he had his worries. There had never been a formal American army, only scattered militias. In his past military experience, Washington had never been in charge of more than thirty men. So he was a bit overwhelmed by the thought of leading many thousands of soldiers and being the one to make decisions that could mean the difference between life and death. Although Washington did not lack confidence in himself, he was naturally a humble and realistic man.

"As Congress desires," Washington said when he accepted his position, "I will enter upon this momentous duty and exert every power I possess in support of this glorious cause . . . but I declare with the utmost sincerity, I do not think myself equal to the command I am honored with."

The members of Congress dismissed Washington's doubts and insisted that he was the man for the job. They also insisted on paying him quite well, but Washington absolutely refused even one penny. He sternly refused to profit from a war.

Before beginning the work of organizing the "Continental Army," as it was named, Washington went home to his estate, Mount Vernon. He and his wife, Martha, were very close, and it pained Washington to realize that he might be away from the woman and the home he loved for many months, perhaps even years. After asking his half-brother, Lawrence, to look after Mount Vernon while he was gone, Washington prepared to head off to war. When they parted, Martha held her husband's hands and admitted that she was frightened for him.

"I foresee consequences," Martha said quietly. "Dark days and darker nights."

George Washington's first days as commander of the Continental Army were not particularly dark, but they were fairly frustrating. Although many men volunteered for service, they knew nothing about the discipline and training needed to form a real army. Most of the volunteers were farmers, who were accustomed to making their own rules and schedules. In addition, because there was no firm age requirement for enlisting, thousands of boys between 15 and 17 years of age rushed to become soldiers. The idea of being a soldier was exciting to these teenagers—the idea of the work involved was not. As a result, Washington was faced with an army of men and boys who were reluctant to follow orders or practice drills.

More than 20,000 men gathered in a camp outside Boston. When Washington took his first look at his new army, he was speechless. The men were housed in filthy tents and crumbling shacks. Because the new recruits considered laundry to be women's work, many of them walked around in clothes that were so dirty they were rotting. The men drank, smoked, and gambled. And there was a serious shortage of guns and an absolute absence of any kind of uniform.

Making matters worse, many of the men constantly quarreled with one another. More often than not, the arguments arose from disagreements between men from very different colonies. A fifteen-year-old recruit from Connecticut named Joseph Plumb Martin later wrote about his experiences:

"They put me in this regiment of half New Englanders and half Pennsylvanians. Folks as different as night and day! And I'd rather be fighting with a tribe of Indians than with these Southerners. I mean, they're foreigners. They can't hardly speak English. They don't like me either. They call me that 'damn Yankee.' And that's about the nicest thing they say."

In the late summer, Washington had to order his men to stop running around naked on the bridge near Cambridge on their way to bathing in the Charles River. More than a few ladies passing over the bridge had been shocked beyond description and had sent furious letters to

Washington. And later that winter, Washington found himself having to break up a fight between Northerners and Southerners. Although it had begun as a 1,000-man snowball fight, it had quickly escalated into a giant fistfight.

"If I could have foreseen what I have and am going to continue to experience," a frustrated Washington wrote in early 1776, "nothing on earth could have persuaded me to take this command."

Nonetheless, Washington was ready to begin defending his country. Nearly 10,000 British troops were still camped in Boston, and in the late winter of 1776, Washington came up with a plan to, hopefully, get rid of them for good. Looking down over Boston and Boston Harbor was an area called Dorchester Heights. For some reason, the British had neglected to secure this area, and now Washington set his sights on it. But what could he place on that hill that would scare the British away? Certainly his ragtag army would not do the trick. In March, a friend of Washington's came to him with an idea.

Henry Knox was a good-natured and very intelligent bookseller from Boston. For many years he had read book after book about military tactics and plans. And for the past few years he had been watching the Redcoats closely, studying their weapons and artillery. He probably knew more about cannons than any other colonist in America. And now cannons were on his mind.

"Fort Ticonderoga," he reminded Washington, "still houses fifty captured cannons. We simply need to move them to Dorchester Heights."

Simply? Washington could not imagine how Knox would move those cannons to Boston. But over the course of two months, Knox accomplished what is considered one of the most remarkable feats of the Revolutionary War. Using sleds pulled by oxen, Knox and a crew dragged fifty cannons over 300 miles of snow-covered mountains. Then, on the night of March 4, 1776, Washington's men hauled the cannons to the top of Dorchester Heights and aimed all fifty at the British troops in Boston.

In the morning, British commander, General William Howe, who had replaced General Gage, looked up at Dorchester Heights through his telescope and then threw his hat down in the dirt in anger.

"These fellows have done more work in one night than I could make my army do in three months!" he bellowed.

Howe didn't know it had actually taken more than two months to place those cannons on the hill, but it didn't really matter. Almost immediately, he ordered all 10,000 of his soldiers to sail out of Boston. There was no way they could fight back against such heavy artillery aimed *down* at them. As Washington and his men watched all the British warships sailing away, there was a lot of whooping and hollering. The Continental Army had driven off the British without firing a shot!

But Washington knew that the British had been scared out of only Boston. There was an entire coastline of other important American ports to invade and attack. So as his men shouted and fired muskets into the air and drank rum, Washington stood silently with his arms folded, watching the disappearing ships. *Where to next?* he wondered.

Not long after the success at Dorchester Heights, John Adams's wife, Abigail, sent a letter to her husband as he attended another meeting of the Second Continental Congress in Philadelphia.

"I long to hear that you have declared an independency," she wrote.

Abigail Adams was anxiously waiting for the second Congress to announce America's independence from England. Until it was written out in a formal statement by Congress and sent to King George, it would not be official. John Adams was just as anxious as his wife, but he urged her to be patient. Of the three million colonists that lived in America, nearly one million of them remained Loyalists. And there were many colonists who still hadn't quite decided which side to take.

"It is all confusion," one colonist from North Carolina explained. "For so long, England has been our mother country. It is hard to think of parting ways."

On the other hand, a woman from New York argued, "How can we play-act and pretend any longer, thinking our brothers in England are willing to listen to us? Freedom is in the hearts and on the lips of us all."

Strange as it may sound, it was a man who had been born and raised in England who, in 1776, persuaded many Americans to support independence from England. Thomas Paine is sometimes even called "The Father of the American Revolution" (a title that is often given to Samuel Adams as well). In England, he had failed at nearly everything he had tried to do: Two marriages, two careers, a few different businesses—nothing ever worked out for Paine. Finally, in 1774, he met an American in London who told him all about the brewing revolution in America. Paine was fascinated and thrilled by the idea of people standing up for what they believed in.

"Why not move there, then?" the American asked. "I'm returning myself. I'll help you get settled."

Paine took his new friend up on the offer. Paine's new American friend was none other than Benjamin Franklin.

Although Paine had been a failure in some areas, he was a good writer. And when he got fired up about something, he was a truly excellent writer. Thomas Paine got very fired up about the idea of independence in America, and in January of 1776 he wrote and published a booklet titled *Common Sense*. A lot of political books and pamphlets of the day were written in difficult language only for the well educated, but Paine wrote his book for the common person in language that anyone could understand.

In *Common Sense*, Paine openly attacked King George, calling him the "Royal Brute of Britain" and making fun of how important the pompous king thought he was. Most important, though, Paine made a strong argument for separating from England:

"Everything that is right or natural pleads for separation. The blood of the slain, the weeping voice of nature cries, ''Tis time to part!' . . . A government of our own is our natural right."

Common Sense was the bestselling publication in America during the entire eighteenth century. Everywhere, people gathered to read it aloud, discuss it, and think about it. Common people working together to create their own government was a new and exciting idea. It had never been done before, and now it fired the imaginations and energies of thousands of colonists.

"I find *Common Sense* is working a powerful change in the minds of many men," said George Washington, who distributed it to his troops and kept a copy close by at all times.

By mid-1776, Paine's little book had had such an effect on readers that the majority of Americans were eagerly pushing the second Congress for a declaration of independence. Now, there was no doubt that it was indeed "time to part."

Paine didn't let his new fame and wealth go to his head. As fall approached, he donated all the money he had made from *Common Sense* to the Continental Army.

"They will need mittens soon," he said with a shrug. When asked how he could give away that much money, Thomas Paine looked confused.

"Why, I do this to honor the cause, of course," he replied.

CHAPTER 6

"What brave fellows I must this day lose!"

*A*s expected, members of the Second Continental Congress vigorously debated whether or not they should formally declare America's independence. Arguments for and against breaking all ties with England went deep into the night for days on end.

"I can scarcely find time to write you a love letter!" John Adams wrote to his wife, Abigail.

Finally, however, twelve of the thirteen colonies agreed to independence. Only New York, where many Loyalists lived, voted against it. Next, the task of actually putting together the formal document was placed in the hands of five members of Congress. Among them were John Adams and a very quiet young man from Virginia named Thomas Jefferson. Jefferson was a skilled architect, a violinist, an inventor, and a master at decoding secret messages. He was, however, not fond of public speaking.

"The whole time I sat next to him in Congress," John Adams once remarked, "I never heard him utter three sentences together."

Jefferson made up for his lack of speaking ability with his talent for writing. Being a modest man, however, Jefferson never thought of himself as a writer talented enough to be the author of the Declaration of Independence. So, when Adams suggested that Jefferson write it, Jefferson tried to change Adams's mind.

"*You* should do it," Jefferson said to Adams.

"Oh! No," Adams said, shaking his head with a smile.

"Why will you not?" Jefferson insisted. "You ought to do it."

"I will not," Adams said.

"But why?" asked Jefferson.

"Reasons enough," Adams replied.

"What can be your reasons?" Jefferson wondered.

Adams looked at Jefferson and grinned. "Reason first—you are a Virginian, and a Virginian ought to appear at the head of this business. Reason second—I am obnoxious and unpopular. You are very much otherwise. Reason third—you can write ten times better than I can."

Jefferson looked a little embarrassed, but he finally nodded and agreed to be the author. Adams smiled and heartily shook his shy friend's hand.

"Good! When you have drawn it up, we will have a meeting," Adams concluded.

For two weeks, Jefferson wrote, made changes, fretted, and paced nervously around his study. He knew how important this document was—this was the official announcement to the entire world of America's intent to separate from England. It had to be worded perfectly. Imagine, then, Jefferson's pain when, on July 3, 1776, all the members of Congress gathered around his carefully written document and began making changes to it.

Ben Franklin took one look at the dismayed Jefferson, and went over and put an arm around Jefferson's shoulder. Franklin led him away from the other members of Congress and told him funny stories, jokes, anything to take Jefferson's mind off what was happening to his document. As it turned out, however, most of the changes were minor.

"We were all in haste," John Adams later explained. "Congress was impatient."

In less than a day, the Declaration of Independence was ready to be signed by the members of Congress. Jefferson had divided the Declaration into two parts. The first part, known as the "preamble," explained why the people of America were justified in wanting to fight against a king and a government that were denying them their natural rights. This preamble was so well written that Congress made no changes to it at all. The preamble's core is expressed in this very famous sentence:

"We hold these truths to be self-evident, that all men are created equal, that they are endowed by their Creator with certain inalienable rights, that among these are life, liberty and the pursuit of happiness."

The second part of the Declaration listed the colonists' grievances, or complaints, about King George. Following these grievances was the official announcement that the colonies would part ways with England. From then on, Congress would begin referring to the colonies as "states"; they would no longer be possessions, or colonies, of England.

Once the final changes were made to the second part of the document, the members of Congress lined up to sign the Declaration of Independence on July 4, 1776. First to sign it was the brash John Hancock, who made his signature unusually large so that King George would notice it right away. To be sure, as the fifty-six signers of the Declaration waited to add their names, they considered the dreadful punishment that they, signed traitors now, would receive if America lost the war. This possible fate was on Ben Franklin's mind as John Hancock handed him the ink quill so that he could add his signature.

"There must be no pulling different ways now," Hancock said sternly to Franklin. "We must all hang together."

"Yes," Franklin said with a wry smile. "We must indeed all hang together, or most assuredly we shall all hang separately."

As the members of the second Congress were signing the Declaration of Independence, George Washington was in the process of moving the Continental Army to New York. Washington had suspected that when the British sailed out of Boston, they would simply head to New York City. It was a powerful port city, and many of the people who lived there were Loyalists, who were glad to house and feed soldiers and officers. However, there were also plenty of Patriots, who were alarmed and angry to see British warships arrive in New York.

On July 2, Washington inspired the Continental Army by having a General Order read to them. The order included these words: "The fate of unborn millions will now depend, under God, on the courage and conduct of this army. . . . We have therefore to resolve to conquer or die. . . . The eyes of all our countrymen are now upon us!"

A week later, Washington had his officers read the Declaration of Independence to their troops. They promptly celebrated by marching into a park in New York City and tearing down a statue of King George. This was the same statue colonists had built to honor the king for his "wise judgment" in doing away with the Stamp Act eleven years earlier. Now the 4,000-pound metal statue was chopped apart and melted down to make bullets for the Continental Army.

The Continental soldiers were excited and confident. They had driven the British army out of Boston; why couldn't they do the same in New York? However, this confidence was dampened a bit in August of 1776. Looking out to sea from his post, the young soldier, Joseph Plumb Martin, recalled seeing what looked like "a forest of timber moving across the water" and toward New York's harbor. These were the tall masts of British ships.

Within days, hundreds of British warships had anchored in the harbor, and many thousands of strange-looking soldiers in tall metal helmets and long braided ponytails began rowing ashore. These were German soldiers known as "Hessians," named for the Hesse region of Germany, where most of them came from. In the 1700s, Germany was a poor country, and to make some money, German leaders had agreed to "lease" their army to England for a modest price. In addition, for every Hessian killed in battle, the German government would receive $22.75, a nice chunk of money in 1776.

Americans were furious. How *dare* King George send in foreign troops! Many Americans who were still trying to decide whether they were for the king or against him made up their minds once the Hessians arrived. It was one thing for King George to send his own troops to kill colonists; it was quite another for him to hire Germans to do his dirty work. Once again, King George's plan backfired. He had thought that the sight of the Hessians would scare Patriots into surrender, but instead it only strengthened their determination to fight.

Following the arrival of the Hessians, many more ships full of British soldiers and artillery and ammunition continued to arrive, until the harbor was jam-packed. By August of 1776, there were tens of thousands of British soldiers in New York—about twice as many British soldiers as Patriots.

"We expect a very bloody summer in New York," Washington wrote frankly to his half-brother. "But I will fight so long as I have a leg or an arm."

The British military did not focus all of its energy on New York, however. General Howe had also sent a small army of Redcoats to

Charleston, South Carolina. In 1776, Charleston was America's third-largest port city, and the British assumed that the unprepared South could easily be conquered and the valuable city of Charleston captured. However, the British were in for a surprise.

Guarding the harbor of Charleston was a rather small militia based on Sullivan's Island, a tiny island at the entrance of the harbor. Leading this militia was Colonel William Moultrie. Moultrie and his men had only twenty-one cannons, and their only protection was a long, low fort constructed of palmetto tree logs and sand.

"It was basically an immense pen filled with sand to stop the shot," one of the Patriot captains explained. As the nine British warships with their 300 cannons approached the island, British officers looked at the fort through their telescopes and laughed out loud. This little American militia with its handful of cannons inside a sand-castle fort wouldn't stand a chance! British commander, Henry Clinton, sent a message to Moultrie offering him the opportunity to surrender before the battle, but Moultrie refused.

With that, the British opened fire from their ships, bombarding Fort Sullivan with a shower of cannonballs. But then an unusual thing happened: Instead of exploding when they hit the fort, the cannonballs sunk deep into the spongy palmetto logs and sand, and fizzled out before they could do any harm. Frustrated British officers ordered their warships to sail closer to the island, but this led only to a number of ships getting stuck on hidden sandbars. Meanwhile, Moultrie and his men continued patiently firing on the British, doing quite a bit more harm to them than the British were doing to the Patriots.

In a final disastrous move, Commander Clinton decided to land his troops on a small uninhabited island barely 100 yards away from Sullivan's Island. From there, the troops planned to wade across the narrow strait between the two islands, and then attack the fort directly. But, as the British troops began wading across, they suddenly disappeared under water. Although Clinton had believed the water to be only eighteen inches deep, it was, in fact, more than seven feet deep with a terribly strong current. The Americans began firing heavily on the floundering British soldiers, killing dozens of them. Finally, Clinton gave up. Angry and humiliated, he ordered the remaining warships (one had exploded when a shot hit its ammunition stores) to head back out to sea. Clinton and his troops would not attempt another attack.

The victory at the Battle of Sullivan's Island was extremely important. It would keep the British away from the South for more than three years, allowing Washington to focus all his energy on the battles in the North. And it convinced many in the Southern states that the British were not as unbeatable as many Patriots feared they were. This, in turn, encouraged many Southerners to volunteer to fight in Washington's Continental Army.

Back in New York, Washington was going to need all the help he could get. Patriot soldiers who were camped on Long Island now slept in their uniforms (if, indeed, they had uniforms), and they kept their guns at their sides. Everyone knew that the British were about ready to pounce. And on August 27, 1776, they did.

"Good God! What brave fellows I must this day lose!" cried Washington as he watched from a nearby hillside. He wrung his hands and paced miserably as the frantic American troops were slaughtered by the British. The Redcoats attacked Long Island from two sides and forced the Patriots further and further into retreat. Finally, after a week of fighting, 1,000 Patriots had been killed, and the Continental Army found itself backed up against the mile-wide East River. They were trapped.

At this point, the British could easily have finished off the Continental Army, but that was not considered "good manners" by the British military. Instead, General Howe ordered his men to fall back and cease firing. Howe assumed that George Washington would surrender within the next day or two; that was the way war was done in Europe.

George Washington, however, was not fighting in Europe, and he had other ideas.

"In the middle of the night, we were all lined up," Joseph Plumb Martin would recall. "We were strictly ordered not to speak, or even cough. All orders were given from officer to officer, and then communicated to the men in whispers."

Boatload by boatload, Patriot soldiers quietly rowed across the East River and over to the island of Manhattan. A small group of soldiers remained in the camp, burning several campfires in hopes that the British would be fooled into believing that nothing out of the ordinary was happening. As morning approached, boats were still shuttling the soldiers across the river. If the British were to see the boats, the Continental Army's escape attempt would be destroyed— along with the army itself, most likely.

But as the sky lightened, an unusually heavy fog clung to the river and along its banks. It completely hid the retreating soldiers. By the time—much later that morning—that the British noticed the American camp to be strangely quiet, all 9,000 Patriot soldiers had escaped.

"In the history of warfare," one American officer wrote, "I do not recollect a more fortunate retreat."

It may have been a fortunate retreat, but it angered and embarrassed the British. *These Americans don't play fair when it comes to war*, the British officers thought. *They should have surrendered!* The Redcoats began pursuing the Continental Army. As the first cold snaps of winter threatened, Washington's outnumbered and outgunned army found itself fighting desperate battles, losing, and then retreating further and further. Some men began losing hope, and many left the army—rather than reenlisting—when their term of service was up.

"I know we must go on," one young soldier sadly wrote to his parents, "but many have now given up. Yesterday I saw my friend beheaded by a twenty-four-pound cannonball. Those Redcoats kill us so easily."

CHAPTER 7

"These are the times that try men's souls"

"*G*eneral Washington's army will not survive the winter," the British commander William Howe said confidently. "There is no need to fight any more battles during these coldest months."

Howe was satisfied to quit pursuing the Continental Army during the winter of 1776–1777. And why shouldn't he be? He and his fellow officers—and even many low-ranking soldiers—were living comfortably in New York City. Wealthy Loyalists had opened their large homes to the British and pampered them with good food, wine, and entertainment. On bitter winter evenings, top British officers could frequently be found sitting by a blazing fire, drinking imported brandy, and watching a play honoring King George put on by Loyalist Americans.

Meanwhile, American soldiers and officers alike sat huddled around small campfires in the snow and sleet. Many of the men were sick and starving, and nearly all of them wore ragged clothing and worn-out shoes. For months, George Washington had sent letters and petitions to the states asking them to send food and clothing to their own regiments. But the states stalled, claiming that the army was now the responsibility of the Second Continental Congress. After all, Congress had chosen the Continental Army's leader.

And so Washington appealed to the second Congress. Congress also dragged its feet, claiming that it could not make decisions for all the states. This kind of runaround made Washington furious. Although Washington was a quiet and thoughtful man, he was known to lose his temper now and then, and during the Revolutionary War, he lost it more than a few times over this issue.

"I am certain," he shot back in an angry letter to Congress, "that unless Congress speaks in a more decisive tone . . . our cause is lost."

Still, no relief came to the American soldiers. As Christmas drew near, many of them were looking forward to the end of the year, when their enlistment would be up. By this point, the Continental Army had retreated all the way to Pennsylvania in its attempt to distance itself from the British. To most of the soldiers, it seemed obvious that the Americans were losing, and they wanted nothing more than to quit and be done with this lost cause.

"The word *surrender* is in every man's head," one soldier wrote in his diary. "Though we dare not speak it, most of us wish to hear it."

Sitting among these weary and hopeless soldiers was Thomas Paine, the author of *Common Sense*. He was there to offer what help and comfort he could to Washington's men, but he soon realized that these soldiers were far beyond the point of being comforted. It was, in a real sense, a time of crisis. If these men all gave up, the British would win. Paine could not bear to see the dream of independence, which had inspired the Patriots barely six months earlier, die so quickly.

Therefore, Thomas Paine did what he did best: He wrote. Since there was no paper in the camp, Paine found a drum and began writing on the bleached leather drumhead:

"These are the times that try men's souls: The summer soldier and the sunshine patriot will, in this crisis, shrink from the service of his country; but he that stands by it now, deserves the love and thanks of man and woman. . . . Tyranny, like hell, is not easily conquered; yet we have this consolation with us, that the harder the conflict, the more glorious the triumph."

George Washington was the first person to read Paine's essay, titled *The Crisis, December 23, 1776*. It reportedly moved him to tears. The end of the year was little more than a week away, and Washington feared that if something drastic didn't happen to change the mood of his soldiers, they would all leave on January 1.

"Ten days more will put an end to the existence of our army," George wrote to his wife, Martha, on December 20.

Due to his grim circumstances, Washington was willing to make a desperate move. Across the Delaware River in Trenton, New Jersey, was a brigade of Hessian soldiers. Most of Trenton was under British control, so the Hessians just helped themselves to the homes there, kicking out families and moving in. Washington knew that the commander of these Hessian troops, Colonel Johann Rall, was not expecting any kind of advance from the American troops.

"Fiddlesticks!" Rall is reported to have said when one British officer warned him to keep an eye out for the Americans. "These clodhoppers will never attack us during the winter."

Washington knew that Rall liked to drink—a lot. Sometimes Rall drank so much that he slept until noon the next day, missing all the morning drills and meetings. Without a doubt, Colonel

Rall and most of his officers would be doing a lot of drinking on Christmas Day. Very late Christmas night, then, Rall and his men would quite likely be asleep in a drunken stupor. Washington decided that this would be the ideal time to surprise the Hessians.

Christmas evening of 1776 was terribly cold. Making matters worse, snow and sleet fell heavily, and great chunks of floating ice bobbed up and down in the Delaware River. Washington gathered his men and read Paine's *The Crisis*. There was, as one soldier put it, a "profound silence" following the reading. Many of the soldiers had tears in their eyes. But there was also new fire in the eyes of many of the Patriots. They would not be "summer soldiers," like those Paine had written about. They would fight on, no matter how bad things got.

Crossing the Delaware that night was rough and dangerous.

"It rained, hailed, snowed, and froze, and at the same time blew a perfect hurricane," a sixteen-year-old soldier remembered.

Some of the small boats seemed likely to turn over in the churning water, and the pounding hail made it nearly impossible for the soldiers to see. George Washington stood on the banks of the river shouting encouragement until three o'clock in the morning. It took that long to ferry more than 2,000 troops and eighteen cannons (again with the help of Henry Knox) across the icy water. And once the river had been crossed, soldiers still needed to march nine miles of frozen road to get to Trenton.

The clothes of most of the soldiers were already soaked from the weather and the river. The men's misery was made complete by the fact that many of them had no shoes, only rags wrapped around their feet. A number of soldiers later commented about the trail of blood that soldiers' feet left along the road to Trenton.

"The wind, the ice—it all cut like a knife," one Patriot said. "The trip there was almost worse than the battle itself."

Washington had hoped to reach Trenton before daylight in order to make the surprise complete, but the terrible weather had delayed the attack. Now, as the sun rose, Washington worried that the Hessian guards would spot the Continental Army and send a warning to Colonel Rall. However, luck was with the Patriots. Rall and his officers had decided, because of the weather and the holiday, to give the guards a night off. Washington and his men marched into Trenton around eight o'clock on the morning of December 26 with no problem.

Knox quickly set up his cannons, and soldiers surrounded the town. With a tremendous boom,

Knox fired the cannons. Within minutes, confused and half-dressed Hessians came stumbling into the streets, their guns in hand. But there was nowhere for the German soldiers to hide and nowhere for them to run. Dozens of Hessians were killed, and 900 were taken prisoner. It was an exceedingly quick battle.

"Hessian population of Trenton at eight a.m.—1,408 men and 39 officers. Hessian population at nine a.m.—zero," one American soldier mockingly announced.

Among the casualties was Colonel Rall. Later that day, as Rall lay dying, his men found a note in his pocket when they removed his bloody shirt. The note was a warning from a Loyalist spy who had seen Washington's men preparing to march to Trenton. When the note had been handed to him on the night of December 25, Rall had been too busy with his party and his card game to pay any attention to it.

"Had I read it when it was delivered, I would not be where I am now," Rall admitted in his final hour.

The American victory at Trenton did the trick. The Continental Army was fired up once again. And it didn't hurt that huge stores of food and clothing were left behind by the defeated Hessians. Now, with coats and new shoes and full stomachs, many of the men who had threatened to go home on January 1 instead signed up for another year of service. Washington used this wave of pride and confidence to rally the men for yet another quick battle. On January 3, the Continentals surrounded and defeated the British in neighboring Princeton, New Jersey.

Back in London, King George was annoyed but not particularly worried. These little victories were, as the king called them, "tiresome," but he was certain the British would finish off Washington's pathetic army once the warmer months of 1777 rolled around. Even as Washington's men were celebrating, King George and his advisers were putting together a new war plan. It was a secret plan that the king was confident would crush the Americans once and for all.

Throughout the states, however, Loyalists were dismayed to learn of the victories in New Jersey. As more and more Americans became devoted to the fight for independence, living in America as a Loyalist became increasingly difficult. New York City was an exception, but in many smaller towns and cities throughout the states, those still loyal to King George were literally run out of town—sometimes at gunpoint. During the winter of 1776–77, Loyalists had truly believed that Washington would give up. Now these "tiresome" victories changed everything.

"A few days ago they had given up the cause for lost," one particularly outspoken Loyalist named Nicholas Cresswell said of Patriot Americans. "Their late successes have turned the scale, and now they are all liberty-mad again!"

As "liberty-mad" as Washington and his army may have been, their enthusiasm brought them no more victories during the spring and summer of 1777. The winter surprise attacks were successful only because the British military did not expect the Americans to break the "rules" of war and fight during the winter months. And as the weather warmed, Washington and the Continental Army broke the rules again.

"These damned Americans!" one British officer complained. "In this country we see the heels of the enemy more than anything else. Washington and his men are cowardly and irregular!"

Washington had discovered that the only way to keep the Revolution alive (and to keep his men alive) was to avoid the British. As Howe and his Redcoats pursued the Americans, the Americans always kept out of reach—just one day ahead of the enemy. The British were far better supplied with weaponry, and their army was significantly bigger. Washington didn't care if they thought he was a coward—fighting back would mean defeat, and defeat would mean the end of the war. So

Washington kept his army on the move, hoping that somehow, some way, the tide would turn in favor of the Americans.

After a few months of this, a frustrated General Howe decided to shift gears and stop chasing the Continental Army. Perhaps, he thought, if the British attacked and captured Philadelphia (often the meeting place of the Continental Congress), the Americans would give up. But even as Howe started planning a raid on the young country's capital city, he and his army reluctantly began to realize that the Americans' desire for independence was stronger than anything else. The Patriots' spirit would not be crushed by battles won or a city captured.

Nonetheless, the Americans needed help; they couldn't keep playing this cat-and-mouse game with the British forever. They needed guns, ships, and more soldiers. In the past, England had supplied the colonists with whatever they needed. Although the Americans had begun to manufacture their own weapons, their arms and ammunition supplies were quickly running out.

Who would help America? The Second Continental Congress met to discuss this, and for once there wasn't much debate about it: France was the obvious choice. The French were still angry about losing to the British in the French and Indian War, and they welcomed any opportunity to get back at England. Even so, it would take some convincing to get the French to side with the Americans. France would not want to join forces with an army that was slowly losing to England. And at the moment, that was exactly what the Americans appeared to be doing.

Choosing the right member of Congress to convince French leaders to help America didn't involve much debate either. The job would require a brilliant, persuasive, and likable man. It was an obvious choice: Benjamin Franklin.

Seventy-one-year-old Franklin, accompanied by his two grandsons, sneaked past the British in Philadelphia and boarded a ship to France. It was a rough trip. For nearly all of the six weeks that it took for the ship to cross the Atlantic Ocean, Franklin was seasick. When he reached France, the carriage that took him to Paris was chased by robbers. And if that were not enough, the French countryside was crawling with British spies. Within hours, Franklin was spotted.

"I learned yesterday that the famous Doctor Franklin has arrived," a spy wrote to his boss in London. "I cannot but suspect that he comes charged with a secret commission from Congress. . . . In a word, I look upon him as a dangerous engine."

After recovering from his exhausting journey, this dangerous engine sent a long letter to the French leader, King Louis XVI. Franklin presented, in some detail, all the reasons why France should want to join forces with America to defeat the British. King Louis reviewed the letter somewhat impatiently, sighing and tapping his fingers as he read. The king had not forgotten that Americans had fought alongside the British in the French and Indian War. And, in many ways, Americans looked and acted very much like the British.

King Louis XVI was not rude to Franklin, but he was not particularly friendly either. After letting Franklin know that, at the moment, the French government was not interested in helping the struggling, outnumbered Americans, the king curtly suggested that Franklin consider returning to America.

But Benjamin Franklin was not about to give up. He would wait for encouraging news from America, and then he would try again to convince King Louis. Franklin realized that that might take some time. Meanwhile, he was in Paris— surrounded by culture, parties, fine champagne, and beautiful women. Franklin wrote to a friend in Philadelphia: "I suppose I will simply have to make the best of it."

And he certainly would.

CHAPTER 8

"A new constellation"

$\mathcal{T}$he King of France may not have been excited about the arrival of Benjamin Franklin, but the French people were thrilled. News of Franklin's inventions and discoveries had traveled to France years earlier, and now Franklin was something of a celebrity. The style-conscious people of Paris had never seen anyone quite like Franklin. He could not have cared less about fashion as he traveled about in his plain old American overcoat and beaver-fur hat. Instead of wearing a powdered wig, he let his stringy brown hair hang down to his shoulders. Despite Franklin's lack of style— or perhaps because of it—women found him irresistible.

"Papa Franklin! Papa Franklin!" came the shouts from young women who followed him down the streets of Paris and demanded that he allow them to kiss his cheek. Women studied his fur hat and then rushed to wigmakers asking for wigs shaped like Franklin's hat. Franklin was the sensation of Paris during the summer of 1777, and he welcomed and encouraged every minute of attention. But it wasn't just that Franklin liked the interest and friendship of the French— he was also working toward a friendship with *France*.

For many months, Franklin accepted nearly every dinner and party invitation he received. And he spent afternoons discussing politics and philosophy with some of the most important men in Paris. Among these men were advisers to King Louis XVI and ministers of foreign relations. Franklin knew that if he could gain the trust and admiration of these men, he might be more successful the next time he asked the king for help. But Franklin would have to be patient. He would need good news of an American victory before he could even consider approaching the king again.

As Franklin socialized and waited, worried British spies swarmed around Paris trying to figure out what Franklin was up to.

"He is the chief of rebels!" one British newspaper said of Franklin. "He is quite a dangerous man."

Eventually, spies broke into Franklin's study.

Much to their horror, they came across some plans and sketches for terrifying and deadly inventions. One invention involved placing gigantic mirrors on the shores of France and aiming them across the English Channel at British ships. It was widely believed that Franklin's mirrors would burn the entire fleet of warships anchored in the Channel.

Franklin's plan for a second invention described a massive chain running from France to England. Connected to this chain would be a tremendous "electrical machine" that could send a shock so terrible that it would flip the entire island of England completely upside down. Needless to say, the discovery of these plans sent tremors of fear throughout Britain. After all, Franklin had discovered electricity. No one doubted that he could create machines that could destroy England.

Back in his study in Paris, Franklin read the stories in British newspapers about the discovery of his proposed inventions. He chuckled and read on. Then he chuckled a little louder. Before he reached the end of the last article, he was laughing so hard that he could barely see through the tears in his eyes. For weeks, Franklin had been well aware that spies had been following him and waiting for a chance to break into his study. He had planted these completely phony "invention plans" on his desk in order to give the British something to worry about.

By midsummer of 1777, King George and his advisers had finished putting together the top-secret plan that they were sure would put an end to this annoying revolution. The idea for the plan had been given to King George by a British general named John Burgoyne. It was simple enough. Burgoyne showed the king a map of the United States and pointed to New York.

"If we can attack from both the north and the south, New York will be ours," Burgoyne explained. "And once we control New York, it will cut New England off from the rest of the colonies."

If this plan succeeded, Northern and Southern states would not be able to share soldiers, supplies, or ammunition. The plan would, in a real sense, take all of the life out of the Revolution. Although the Americans were suffering as they fought this lopsided war, at least they were able to keep the war going by working together. If the North and the South were separated, the Patriots would be unable to continue.

King George put Burgoyne in charge of the invasion from the north. Burgoyne and his army would travel south from Quebec, Canada, while General Howe and his men would travel north from New York City. The two forces would meet in Albany, New York, attacking towns and settlements along the way until New York was entirely in British hands.

Burgoyne was so sure that his plan would work that he bet a friend fifty pieces of gold that he could conquer the Americans and be back in London within one year. That was quite an ambitious bet. It meant that within one year Burgoyne would have to cross the Atlantic, organize his army in Quebec, march all the way to Albany, beat the Continental Army, return to New York City, and sail back to England. But Burgoyne was confident. He had heard how small and poorly equipped Washington's army was, and he knew that if he combined forces with Howe, there was no way the Americans could win.

It was with this air of overconfidence that Burgoyne prepared for his time in America. In many ways, he seemed to look at going to war as something similar to going on vacation. On board his ship, he had many cases of champagne and gourmet foods for picnics along the scenic route from Quebec to Albany. The wives of nearly all his officers had also decided to join this adventure to keep their husbands company. It was not uncommon for the wives of top officers to travel with their husbands; Martha

Washington often spent the winter months with George Washington near the Continental Army's camp. However, several hundred women traveling with their officer husbands was quite unusual.

Once Burgoyne reached Canada, he needed a few weeks to get everything ready for the long march to Albany. Many of the women had taken numerous trunks of clothing, accessories, and wigs. The women's belongings, along with Burgoyne's supply of fancy foods, filled more than thirty wagons, which would have to be hauled hundreds of miles! While this seemed ridiculous to many of Burgoyne's soldiers, they certainly didn't mind the good food that their general often shared with them. John Burgoyne loved spoiling his soldiers and, as a result, he was affectionately nicknamed "Gentleman Johnny" by his troops.

Even as Gentlemen Johnny was putting the finishing touches on his army's elaborate travel plans, George Washington was receiving word of this "top-secret" British plan from Patriot spies. It seems that all secrets became public during the Revolution. Both sides often went to great lengths to send messages in code, only to have secret agents discover the plans anyway. Because it was often difficult to tell the difference between British people and Americans, it was quite easy for spies to slip into enemy camps, mingle with soldiers, and come away with all kinds of juicy information.

In any event, Washington became worried. He had thought (thanks to another spy) that General Howe was planning an attack on Philadelphia. But now it sounded as though Howe was going to meet Burgoyne in Albany. What should Washington do? Which plans would Howe follow? Finally Washington decided to keep the Continental Army near Philadelphia. Washington may have run from other battles with the British, but he would not allow them to take over America's capital city without a fight. Another smaller American force, the Northern Army, would have to handle the battle in Albany. To help lead this army, Washington picked a merchant from Connecticut named Benedict Arnold.

"General Arnold didn't care about nothing except fighting," one soldier said. "He'd ride right in without a worry in the world. No, sir— you wouldn't want to be on that general's bad side."

Benedict Arnold wasn't a very likable leader. He was loud, easily angered, bossy, and argumentative. But he was brave and, Washington fully believed, 100 percent devoted to the Revolution.

"We have one advantage over the enemy," Arnold had once written: "It is in our power to be free, or nobly die in defense of liberty."

Washington liked that. He put his faith in Arnold and sent him north to serve as second-in-command to the top general, Horatio Gates. Gates, an older and less aggressive general, often thought Arnold was an obnoxious hothead. Arnold, on the other hand, thought Gates was a timid old man who was afraid of fighting. Some of Gates's soldiers had nicknamed him "Granny Gates" because of his age and because of the way he wore his glasses on the end of his nose. Benedict Arnold was more than happy to use this unflattering name behind the general's back.

Nonetheless, the two generals would have to work together. The first decision they made was to march the Northern Army to the town of Saratoga, New York, instead of Albany. Saratoga was just north of Albany, and the generals hoped that the army's presence there would catch the British off-guard. In addition, Saratoga was better suited for building the forts that would protect the soldiers during battle. So, as autumn approached, American soldiers began preparing for what looked as though it would be the biggest battle yet.

Although the men worked terribly hard to get ready for the Battle of Saratoga, their spirits were not at their best. There had been no victories; supplies were running low; and it looked as though no other country was going to come to America's aid.

There was, however, one thing that made the men feel a certain sense of pride and unity: a new national flag. Up until 1777, Americans had flown what was known as "the Grand Union Flag," a flag that resembled the flags of other British-ruled colonies. But now Americans wanted something to symbolize their independence. Soldiers began asking for a new flag to wave as they went into battle.

The Second Continental Congress met and came up with a design in the summer of 1777.

"Resolved," Congress put into writing, "that the flag of the United States be thirteen stripes, alternate red and white; that the union be thirteen stars, white in a blue field, representing a new constellation."

The story goes that a young woman named Betsy Ross sewed the very first flag. Supposedly, Ross came up with a design for stars with five points, instead of the six that Congress had asked for, because they were easier to sew. When she showed the stars to George Washington, he was reported to have been so impressed with the design that he personally asked Ross to make the first flag.

This may or may not be true. For one thing, there are no written records to support the idea that Betsy Ross sewed the first flag; the story was simply passed along by Ross's grandson, who had heard the story from his aunt. In reality, six or seven women were given the task of putting together the American flag. Some records back up the idea that Ross had the idea of a five-pointed star, but there is no proof that she "made" the first flag. Still, Americans liked the story, and whether it was fact or legend did not seem to matter much. More than 200 years later, Betsy Ross is still often honored as the woman who sewed the first flag.

And it was this flag that flew for the first time as American soldiers anxiously awaited the arrival of Burgoyne in Saratoga. The Northern Army had been late in getting everything prepared for battle, but, luckily, Burgoyne had been even later. At first, things had gone well for Burgoyne. He had easily recaptured Fort Ticonderoga in northern New York from the Americans. And as he traveled, he convinced large bands of Iroquois Indians both to fight with him and to help him find paths through the confusing dense forests.

The Iroquois were, understandably, reluctant to help the British. However, Burgoyne convinced them that if the British won, the British king would put an end to Americans expanding westward and taking over Native American lands. It is doubtful that King George would have done anything of the kind, but the Iroquois believed Burgoyne, and they joined his army. Burgoyne was ecstatic. He knew how terrified Americans were of Indians. Perhaps, when these annoying Patriots saw the Iroquois marching with the British, they would simply surrender without a fight at all.

However, once again, the British attempt to frighten the Americans backfired. When a young woman named Jane McCrea was scalped and killed by several Iroquois, the news spread quickly, and the gruesome details of the murder became more and more exaggerated. In no time at all, dramatic songs were written about the "lovely and brilliant" McCrea, and she was celebrated and remembered in paintings and literature. Jane McCrea's death became a rallying cry to fight Burgoyne, and suddenly thousands of New Yorkers joined in the effort to defeat Gentleman Johnny and his men.

Not surprisingly, when the Iroquois realized what a hornet's nest they had stirred up, they decided to return home and have nothing more to do with this Revolutionary War. Now John Burgoyne and his army were left alone to navigate the muddy and vague paths through northern New York. It was at this point that

Burgoyne really began to regret having thirty wagons full of fancy foods and officers' wives' wigs and clothes. Wheels got stuck in the mud, paths came to dead ends, and soldiers complained about mosquitoes. Making matters worse, New York Patriots placed boulders on the paths, burned bridges, and flooded roadways in an attempt to slow Burgoyne down.

Finally, Burgoyne and his army were able to cover barely a mile a day. In Saratoga, Benedict Arnold and Horatio Gates took advantage of this precious extra time by making battle plans— or, at least, arguing about battle plans. As more and more men kept streaming in to volunteer for the Battle of Saratoga, it occurred to Arnold that the Americans could charge head-on into Burgoyne's army and, possibly, overtake them at once. Gates could not have disagreed more strongly. Gates felt it would be better to keep the Patriot soldiers inside the fort, where they would be protected as they fired from behind log walls.

By now, naturally, Burgoyne had received word that the Americans were waiting for him at Saratoga and that the Northern Army had grown in size as the British army had shrunk. Still, Burgoyne was confident. He knew that he would receive word from General Howe any day. Howe's march north from New York

City would certainly have taken less time than Burgoyne's march south from Quebec. In fact, Burgoyne thought, Howe and his huge army were probably already positioned just south of Saratoga. Burgoyne and his men would merely have to meet up with Howe and then close the trap on the Northern Army. This thought made Burgoyne smile.

Not two days before Burgoyne was to reach Saratoga, however, his smile faded. A brief and rather terse message arrived from Howe, who had never had much respect for Gentleman Johnny. There would be no army coming north to help. Howe and his men had decided to attack Philadelphia instead.

Burgoyne was stunned and furious.

"When I had been more confident," Burgoyne later wrote in his defense, "I had not foreseen that I was to be left to pursue my way through such a tract of country and host of foes, without any cooperation from New York!"

Some of Burgoyne's officers suggested that the army return to Canada. But Burgoyne couldn't bear the thought of giving up. If his army could fight its way around Saratoga and escape to Albany, there were enough Loyalists there to house the army over the winter. Then, in the spring, the fighting could resume. Most of Burgoyne's officers were skeptical.

"In truth," one officer admitted, "I had never heard a worse plan. It was as if the general had lost all sense."

In any event, it was beginning to look like John Burgoyne was going to lose his bet of fifty gold coins.

CHAPTER 9

"This army will starve, dissolve, or disperse!"

"*R*ush on, my brave boys! Rush on!"

The hoarse shouts of Benedict Arnold pierced the booms of the cannons and the roar of the rifles. Arnold had finally worn Gates down in their argument about how to attack Burgoyne's army. Now he charged directly into the British as they approached Saratoga, leading his men from the front, and shouting encouragement nonstop.

"Arnold rushed into the thickest of the fight with his usual recklessness," one officer later commented. "At times, he acted like a madman."

Both sides seemed determined to win, and the fighting was some of the most vicious yet seen in the Revolution. Although the Americans outnumbered the British, General Burgoyne refused to allow his men to retreat. He was determined to get to Albany for the winter. And in keeping with his typically overblown confidence,

Burgoyne assumed that this ragged American army—regardless of its number of men—could never actually defeat his well-trained, brightly uniformed troops.

And so the battle continued until it became too dark to aim guns and cannons. Nearly a thousand soldiers had been wounded or killed, including dozens of Burgoyne's best officers. Still, Burgoyne wanted to head right back into battle the very next morning. His men, however, refused. They needed time to recover and heal a bit. Reluctantly, Burgoyne decided to hold his position and reinforce the camp while his men regained their strength. Burgoyne still firmly believed that help must be on the way. Surely, General Howe's army—or at least *part* of his army—would arrive to help out. Burgoyne thought that, at the very least, another British regiment must have been assigned to reinforce his army.

However, days passed—and no help arrived. The Americans waited impatiently for Burgoyne to either make his move or surrender. Gates and Arnold continued bickering over plans for the next battle, and soldiers lay awake listening to wolves howling on the battlefield. Shallow graves for killed soldiers had been hastily dug, and now hungry timber wolves dug up bodies and ate them.

"It was ghastly," one American officer recalled. "Nights when the moon was bright, we could see the wolves in packs at their work. It is a nightmare I'm not soon to forget."

Three weeks passed, and Burgoyne was becoming desperate. Clearly, Howe had no intention of sending help, and now food and supplies were nearly gone. Finally, on October 7, 1777, Burgoyne and his army attacked again, but this time the fighting ended long before sunset. It was a clear American victory, complete with Benedict Arnold defying General Gates's orders to remain off the battlefield. In a fury fueled by patriotism (and possibly alcohol), Arnold had stormed out onto the battlefield waving his rifle and screaming, "Liberty or death!" Although this inspired many of the soldiers, it was not the wisest move. Within minutes, Arnold was shot in the leg and had to be hauled back to camp, where an angry Horatio Gates gave him no sympathy.

Now Burgoyne retreated, worried, schemed, and finally decided to attempt a midnight escape from Saratoga. The escape didn't work. The Americans surrounded the British and waited for them to surrender. Burgoyne was unwilling to do this—until it occurred to him that if he did not give up, he would have to watch his men starve. On October 17, Gentleman Johnny put on a clean uniform, powdered his wig, and walked out across the battlefield with 5,700 unarmed soldiers in a formal display of surrender. Lining the hillsides, thousands of American soldiers watched quietly, their hats in their hands as a show of respect for the beaten enemy.

"Not one of them was properly uniformed!" griped one bitter British soldier. "Each man had on the clothes in which one goes to the field, the church, or the tavern."

But many of the British soldiers noticed something much more important than the Americans' clothes: They saw a certain pride and strength and determination in the faces of the Patriots. It was something the British had never seen before.

"I felt as though I was looking at a new race of men," a British officer would later write.

The American victory at Saratoga was huge. It would soon become known as the turning point of the American Revolution. When the news reached Paris about a month later, Benjamin Franklin immediately made plans to visit King Louis XVI. How could the king refuse to support the Americans after such a spectacular defeat of the British?

Franklin rushed to the gates of Versailles, the king's palace, but he was abruptly blocked from entering.

"Sir, it is strongly suggested that one wear a wig when addressing the king," a guard said, eyeing Franklin's bald head with some disgust.

Franklin sighed. But if it took a fancy white wig to gain admission to the king, a fancy white wig was what he would wear. Naturally, half the population of Paris waited eagerly to see how Franklin's wig would turn out. It didn't turn out well. The wigmaker made it about two sizes too small for Franklin's rather large head.

"It is true that Franklin does have a fat head," a Paris newspaper instantly reported. "But it is a great head."

Franklin did not want to wait another two days for a larger wig. He would take his chances appearing before King Louis with his fat bald head. Luckily, the king barely even looked at Franklin. He had already made up his mind about helping America, and he kept his one comment brief.

"Assure Congress of my friendship," King Louis said politely. "I hope this will be for the good of the two nations."

Success! All of Franklin's time spent in Paris talking with officials and advisers, keeping interest in the American Revolution alive, and working to keep a connection to King Louis had paid off. Now Franklin was free to return home to Philadelphia—but Franklin was in no hurry. He had come to love the French as much as they loved him, and now he was in the middle of learning both the French language and the art of winemaking. How could he leave? As it turned out, Benjamin Franklin would not return to America for another eight years.

The news of promised French support reached America just as the winter of 1777 was beginning to get ugly. Certainly, George Washington was excited and encouraged by this news, but he knew that help from France would not arrive in any major way until the spring. And his Continental Army needed help very badly right now.

"To see men without clothes to cover their nakedness, without blankets to lie on, without shoes, by which their marches might be traced by the blood from their feet," Washington wrote that winter, "is a proof of patience and obedience which in my opinion can scarce be paralleled."

The soldiers in Washington's army may have been patient and obedient, but they were very unhappy. Just as the snow began piling up in Pennsylvania, these weary, hungry men were ordered to march to an area known as Valley Forge and build a brand new camp on a frozen, barren plain. A few months earlier, General Howe and his army had indeed attacked Philadelphia, and now the city was under British control. Washington and his officers agreed that it would be best for the Continental Army to remain close to Philadelphia during the winter to keep an eye on it. Valley Forge, only twenty miles from Philadelphia, seemed like a good location.

It is hard to imagine just how badly Washington's army suffered during the winter of 1777. In temperatures well below freezing, many of the men went about the camp wearing no more than thin, moth-eaten blankets around their bare shoulders. For nearly a month, until log huts were constructed, soldiers lived in tents that were covered with ice. To keep their feet from freezing solid, soldiers who were assigned guard duty often stood on their hats in the snow—only to receive frostbite on their ears. By late December, more than 5,000 men (nearly half the army) had fallen ill from the cold. Many had to have feet and legs, blackened by frostbite, amputated.

But as bad as the bitter cold was, the hunger was worse. The soldiers often went for days at a time with nothing to eat but cold water and "fire bread"—hard, tasteless bread made by mixing water and flour and then charring the watery dough over coals.

"I don't doubt our guts have turned to pasteboard!" one soldier wrote after weeks of a steady diet of fire bread.

Finally, even the fire bread ran out.

"I swear that I did not put a single morsel into my mouth for four days and as many nights," the young soldier Joseph Plumb Martin recalled, "except a little black birch bark which I gnawed off a stick of wood. I saw several of the men roast their old shoes and eat them."

And when Martin and his comrades received their Christmas dinner—half a cup of rice and a tablespoonful of vinegar—Martin could barely contain his fury in his diary entry:

"We are now absolutely in danger of perishing in the midst of a plentiful country . . . in whose service we are wearing away our lives."

Washington and his officers did not suffer the cold and starvation that winter, since most of them lived in houses and buildings in the towns surrounding Valley Forge. But Washington suffered terribly when he rode through the camp and saw his men. More than once, he lost his temper in letters to the Second Continental Congress.

"Unless some great change suddenly takes place," he wrote angrily, "this army will starve, dissolve, or disperse! Rest assured, this is not an exaggerated picture."

The summer of 1777 had been mild, and the crops had been unusually plentiful for American farmers. In addition, approximately 75,000 farmers lived within fifty miles of Valley Forge. How could it be, then, that none of this food was getting to Washington's army? Some of the blame lay with lack of organization. An army of many thousands of men was a new thing for America. No one knew exactly how to transport tons of food from farms, ports, or factories out to a field camp. And some of the blame, as before, lay with confusion (or stubbornness) over whether responsibility for the soldiers' care lay with the second Congress or with the states.

But there was another reason that food was not getting to Washington's army—and Washington called this a "national disgrace": Many businessmen withheld food and clothing from soldiers because they could get more money for their goods elsewhere. These same businessmen sometimes even waited to sell their supplies until the army became desperate and was willing to pay higher prices.

Washington felt that those who engaged in this kind of business should be shot and killed.

"No punishment, in my opinion, is too great for the man who can build his greatness upon his country's ruin," Washington bitterly wrote to Congress during that long winter at Valley Forge. But very little relief ever came. Before the winter ended, nearly 2,000 men had died of disease, hunger, and cold—far more than had been killed in battle up to that point in the war.

However, as the spring of 1778 approached, things slowly began to look up. Washington received word that French troops and ships full of supplies would be arriving soon. In addition, a number of European military leaders began appearing at American camps. Many Europeans were fascinated by the idea of a young country standing up to the mighty British and fighting for its freedom. One of these Europeans was an elderly man from Prussia named Friedrich Wilhelm August Heinrich Ferdinand von Steuben.

It was rumored that von Steuben made up his unusually long name in order to sound important. He also invented some of his military history to impress Washington, claiming that he had been friends with Frederick the Great and had fought under the legendary king of Prussia. Washington didn't care about fancy names or histories, but he was impressed by von Steuben's ability to train soldiers. Von Steuben may have been two or three times older than most of the soldiers in the Continental Army, but he had endless energy, and knowledge about drills and exercises. Until Von Steuben came along, no one in the Continental Army—not even Washington—had really known how to train soldiers. When Washington first gave Von Steuben a tour of the troops during their "exercises," the old man's face turned red with anger, and he swore loudly in German. He had never before seen such disorganized, sloppy soldiers.

"Your men may be brave," von Steuben told Washington through a translator, "but they are untrained."

For the remainder of the spring months, von Steuben blasted the soldiers out of bed with a bugle call at three o'clock in the morning. Until well after sunrise, the soldiers learned how to march in formation, take orders, reload their guns with precision, and work together as a strong unified force. Von Steuben was famous for losing his temper and asking his translator to swear at the men in English. By the end of May, however, the Continental Army had changed. The men were proud of their new skills, and when they finally got money for uniforms, many of the men felt like true soldiers for the first time. Although they'd had a terrible winter, they now felt eager to take on the British.

The British, however, were not so enthusiastic. Howe and his army had spent a fairly comfortable winter in Philadelphia, taking over the homes of the city's residents—and eating their food and drinking their wine. One officer, John André, had even stayed in Benjamin Franklin's house.

Reportedly, André had spent much of the winter going through Franklin's scientific instruments, artwork, and personal papers—and then packing them up and taking them with him when he left.

By the time the British left Philadelphia, their plans had changed. No longer would they waste time, supplies, and energy chasing Washington and the Continental Army all over the northeast. Now that France had entered the war, it was a different war altogether. France and England had been enemies for nearly a century, and now France was looking to fight the British wherever they could—not only in America. The French were happy to battle the British in Europe or even in the Bahamas, where Britain owned a number of very valuable sugar-producing islands. Making matters even worse for the British, Spain had sided with France and vowed to do everything possible to help the French in America and beyond.

The British were becoming very frustrated. This relatively unimportant little war with misbehaving colonists had now expanded to a worldwide war. Instead of just focusing on beating the Americans (something they had originally thought they could do quickly), the British now had to place their military in numerous locations around the world. Clearly, the British were no longer interested in playing cat and mouse with George Washington.

Meanwhile, Washington surveyed his troops with their new skills and their new confidence. He knew they were itching to fight. And as spring turned to summer, the soldiers grew impatient.

"When are we going after the Redcoats?" soldiers shouted as Washington rode through the camp. "Let's go!"

By late June, there had still been no attack by the Redcoats. It had become clear to Washington that the British were through with chasing the Continental Army. It was time, then, for the Americans to chase the British.

CHAPTER 10

"Who knows what fortune will do for us?"

Soldiers in the Continental Army had never heard George Washington swear, but on June 28, 1778, they heard him use some choice words when speaking angrily to one of his generals. Washington had thought he and his officers had come up with the perfect plan for defeating the British army. General Howe had grown so frustrated with the war that he had decided to quit and go back home to England. The Redcoats were now led by General Henry Clinton, the same general who had lost the Battle of Sullivan's Island near Charleston in 1776. Washington saw an advantage with this newer and less-experienced general in charge. And word had reached Washington that Clinton was now leading his army out of Philadelphia toward New York City.

Washington laid the trap and was ready to pounce on the British army near Monmouth, New Jersey. Unfortunately, Washington had placed a young general named Charles Lee in charge of leading the attack. Washington was not happy with giving Lee this responsibility, but he didn't have much of a choice of generals at the time. Additionally, Lee was a fairly high-ranking general, and he insisted on being given the task.

Lee had the reputation of being something of an oddball. He frequently claimed that he didn't even like people and preferred the company of dogs instead. Lee often took his pack of poorly trained hounds to dinner parties or afternoon teas. Although Lee liked fancy uniforms, he refused to wash them, regularly wearing the same uniform for months at a time. Some soldiers claimed that Lee's dogs smelled better than he did. Worst of all, Lee made it very clear that he didn't think much of George Washington as a leader.

"Washington isn't fit even to be a sergeant!" Lee once remarked loudly at a party attended by a number of Continental Army officers.

Washington was aware of Lee's bad attitude, but he figured that a top general, regardless of his poor reputation, could certainly lead the attack against the British. Lee was given specific and fairly simple instructions about leading the army into battle. All he had to do was follow them—

but he didn't. Instead, Lee allowed the soldiers to fight for an hour or so, and then, for unexplainable reasons, he ordered a complete retreat. When Washington saw his army returning, he rushed out to meet Lee.

"General Lee! What are you doing?" Washington shouted.

Lee just looked at Washington and said, "What?"

"What is the reason for this disorder and confusion?" Washington demanded, pointing at the retreating men.

"The American troops would not stand the British bayonets," Lee said sulkily, refusing to meet Washington's stare.

At that point, Washington blew up. "You damned poltroon [coward]!" he bellowed. "You never even tried them!"

After calling Lee a few more unusual names, Washington did his best to rally the soldiers back into battle. It was too late for a real victory, however. Both sides fought until sunset, and finally the British retreated first. Although the battle had no clear winner, the Americans had made quite an impression. The newly trained Continental Army had surprised the British with its organization and precision. This was no longer a weak collection of untrained militias—this was a real army.

Perhaps the most interesting story to come out of the Battle of Monmouth was the legend of Molly Pitcher. A young woman named Mary Hays had joined her husband, William, at Valley Forge as winter came to a close. She, along with other soldiers' and officers' wives, tended to the army's needs by mending clothes, cooking, and helping the sick. As the weather grew warmer, some of these women, known as "camp followers," often took pitchers of water out to the men as they practiced drills.

The most popular name for a woman in the 1700s was "Mary," and the most common nickname for Mary was "Molly." As the days got hotter and the work became harder, soldiers often shouted for water by calling, "Molly! Pitcher!" In time, then, many of these women who aided soldiers became known as "Molly Pitcher." In other words, Mary Hays was not the only "Molly Pitcher" during the Revolution, but she was the most famous one following the Battle of Monmouth.

William Hays was working the cannon crew that day as his wife regularly rushed out into the battle to deliver water to the men. Temperatures hovered near 100 degrees, and many men were fainting and even dying of heatstroke. Suddenly, William Hays collapsed. Mary quickly tended to her husband and then jumped up, shook her fist at the British, and took over William's job of firing the cannon. The young soldier, Joseph Plumb Martin, saw what happened next:

"While in the act of reaching for a cartridge and having one of her feet as far before the other as she could step, a cannon shot from the enemy passed directly between her legs without doing any other damage than carrying away all the lower part of her petticoat."

The story of Mary Hays caused quite a sensation. Most Americans could not imagine a woman even getting near the fighting, much less firing a cannon in the middle of it. However, Hays was certainly not the only woman to enter the battlefield during the Revolution. It is estimated that there were several thousand female camp followers. Many hundreds of these women dodged bullets to aid soldiers, and, on occasion, they did indeed shoot back at the British.

"I'm not afraid of the cannonballs," a camp follower named Sarah Osborn once said to George Washington when he asked her if she was ever frightened when delivering food to the men on the battlefield. "It would not be right for the men to fight and starve, too," Osborn simply stated.

Of course, women were not allowed to enlist, but some found ways to become soldiers, regardless of the rules. Perhaps the most famous was a young woman named Deborah Sampson. Sampson was determined to fight for her country, so she disguised herself as a man (even her own mother didn't recognize her!) and signed up as "Robert Shurtliff" from Massachusetts.

Sampson was, apparently, both an excellent soldier and a master of disguise. She fought with the infantry in several battles without raising a bit of suspicion. When she was shot twice in the leg, she refused treatment, worried that doctors would find out she was a woman. Instead, Sampson used a knife and a sewing needle to dig out the musket balls; then she returned to the war. Eventually, Sampson's gender was discovered by a doctor treating her for a high fever, but when it was reported to her commanding officer, she was not punished. Though she had broken the law, she was so admired for her service and bravery that she was given an honorable discharge.

Other women worked as spies. When the British occupied Philadelphia in 1777, British officers held meetings in the home of Lydia Darragh. Because the Darragh family was Quaker (a religious group that did not believe in participating in war), the British believed they were safe meeting in the Darragh house. However, they were wrong. Lydia was a strong supporter of American independence and routinely hid behind doors, listening to the British. More than once, Lydia Darragh wrote about British plans in simple code, hid the messages in her clothing, and managed to get the information to General Washington.

Nonetheless, the vast majority of women who helped during the Revolution did not play such daring and exciting roles. More commonly, women gathered in large groups to sew uniforms, make food, and even raise money for the troops. Countless women opened their homes to American soldiers and officers during the bitter winter months, feeding them and taking care of them until summer arrived.

And as thousands of women worked hard for their country's independence, some women began thinking about their own freedoms. True, they supported this new Declaration of Independence that announced that "all men are created equal." But what about fairness for women? In the 1700s, even thinking about equality for women was considered strange and somewhat shocking. Women were supposed to stay out of politics, keep quiet, and take care of the home and the family. But some women refused to remain silent. Abigail Adams, the wife of John Adams, was one such woman.

"I desire you would remember the ladies and be more generous and favorable to them than your ancestors," Abigail had said in a letter to John when the Declaration was being written. "Do not put such unlimited power into the hands of the husbands. Remember, all men would be tyrants if they could. If particular care and attention is not paid to the ladies, we are determined to start a rebellion, and will not hold ourselves bound by any laws in which we have no voice or representation."

Unfortunately, John's response to his wife was "As to your extraordinary laws, I cannot help but laugh."

To this, Abigail shot back, "While you are proclaiming peace and good will to men, emancipating all nations, you insist upon retaining an absolute power over wives!"

John and Abigail continued to debate this issue privately in their "love letters" to one another. However, a number of women in the mid-1700s expressed their opinions publicly. During the war, at least six women attempted to share their views and ideas through newspapers they published. These newspapers may not have resulted in any drastic changes, but they got women thinking. Then thinking turned to action when women began demanding the right to vote. As it turned out, women would not be granted that right for nearly 150 years. However, the first seeds of the struggle for women's rights were planted during the American Revolution.

• • •

After the Battle of Monmouth, the British decided to focus their efforts elsewhere in America. For two years they had chased Washington and the Continental Army around the northeast. And now the first attack by Washington had resulted in a stalemate. It was time for the British army to direct their energy toward other parts of the country. The first place they turned was the unsettled area west of the thirteen states, an area known as "the frontier."

Many Americans were beginning to explore and settle the lands beyond the East. Years earlier, King George had issued a proclamation forbidding colonists to move west into already-settled Indian Territory. It wasn't that the king was particularly concerned about the rights of Native Americans; he just didn't want to deal with what he knew would be a bloody and expensive war. However, many people ignored the king's proclamation. They were curious about what lay beyond the Allegheny Mountains, and they were tired of living in the crowded towns and cities in the East.

Now the British saw an opportunity. As General Burgoyne had done, the British convinced these western Indians that the Americans were the enemy.

"These rebels cut down your trees, make roads, and take your lands away from you for their farms," British officers explained to the natives. "Help us conquer them. Fight with us, and your lands shall remain forever yours."

The Indians were not easily convinced.

The Native Americans of the frontier were made up of Indians from the Mohawk, Oneida, Cayuga, Seneca, Onondaga, and Tuscarora tribes, but centuries earlier, they had realized that they could be stronger if they all worked together. As one unified group, they called themselves "the Iroquois." Some of these same Iroquois had been swayed by General Burgoyne a year earlier, and that had not turned out well at all. Now these Iroquois argued against siding with the British again. Others, however, felt it was worth doing anything to get rid of the Americans, who were stealing land from them.

Although these six tribes, known as "the Six Nations," had been a mighty unified force for more than 300 years, the American Revolution pulled these Native Americans apart. After much debate—some of it very bitter—four tribes chose to side with the British, and two with the Americans.

The British wasted no time with their advantage. They gave the Iroquois guns and knives, and encouraged them to be as brutal as possible when attacking Americans.

As before, the British hoped the Indians

would scare the American settlers on the frontier so badly that they would back down and give up the fight. And for a while, their plan appeared to be working. The thing that terrified settlers the most was the Iroquois practice of scalping. Obtaining a scalp was a horribly bloody and gruesome procedure that usually left its victim dead. Contrary to popular myth, most Native Americans did not scalp their enemies, but during the Revolution, some Iroquois did. And British officers, unfortunately, made this practice more common by offering the Iroquois cash rewards for scalps. One officer in particular, Colonel Henry Hamilton, was nicknamed "the Hair Buyer," because he collected so many scalps.

When these stories of scalping and torturing reached England, they did not have the effect the British military had hoped for. Many British people were horrified and angered by what was happening.

"What are we doing, in the name of God?" a member of Parliament asked. "We have given permission to these Indians to behead, to burn, to dismember our brothers in America! For what purpose, I know not."

In what would later become the state of Kentucky, a twenty-five-year-old settler named George Rogers Clark refused to back down in fear. In February of 1779, Clark gathered 170 frontiersmen and set off in search of Hamilton, the Hair Buyer. When Hamilton received word that Clark was headed his way, he put together an army of 500 men and positioned them at a well-built fort in Vincennes, Indiana. While Clark and his men struggled to march across 180 miles of frozen frontier, Hamilton and his soldiers just sat back and waited. And while they waited, more than 200 Iroquois came to Vincennes to join the Hair Buyer at the fort.

Things were not looking good for Clark and his small militia. Still, Clark remained positive.

"I know the case is desperate," Clark wrote in a letter during the march. "But who knows what fortune will do for us? Great things have been affected by a few men well conducted. Perhaps we may be fortunate. We have this consolation— that our cause is just, and that our country will be grateful."

As it turned out, fortune would do great things for Clark. When he and his men approached the town of Vincennes, Clark decided to try a bit of trickery: Because the main street of the town was built on a slope that disappeared behind a hill, Clark was able to march his men right down Main Street in two columns, have them swing back through side streets, and then march down Main Street again. They did this over and over. Basically, the soldiers were just walking in circles, but to observers in both the town and the fort, it appeared that Clark had a thousand men or more. Guards rushed to the Hair Buyer and warned him that the British were terribly outnumbered.

When the shooting began, the British were no match for these frontier-trained sharpshooters, who had been hunting for years.

"It was nothing for me and my brother to shoot a squirrel right in the eye from a hundred yards away," one of Clark's men bragged after the battle.

The frontiersmen picked off dozens of British soldiers who cowered and tried to hide behind the walls of the fort. Hamilton now truly believed that Clark must have 1,000 men fighting with him. Before the sun began to set that day, Hamilton, the Hair Buyer, sent out a soldier with a white flag of surrender. Instantly, Hamilton was captured and sent to prison, and Britain's biggest fort on the frontier became an American possession.

When the new British general, Henry Clinton, heard of this surprising upset, he was nearly speechless with anger. How on earth could this have happened? With Fort Vincennes taken by the Americans, there was no point in keeping British troops on the frontier. He ordered most of them to return to New York. In frustration, he met with his officers. What should they do next? The British could not seem to make any headway in the Northeast, and now they had lost the frontier.

Only one option remained: It was time to head south again.

CHAPTER 11

"Whom can we trust now?"

*W*hen the Second Continental Congress heard that the British were headed south to the Carolinas and Georgia, it decided to put General Horatio Gates in charge of the American army in the South. This seemed like a good idea. After all, he was considered the hero of the Battle of Saratoga. He had led his army to an unlikely victory once; perhaps he could do it again. Everyone agreed that Gates was the best choice. Rather *almost* everyone agreed.

In Philadelphia, Benedict Arnold was still recovering from the wounds he had received at Saratoga. The bullets had shattered a bone in his leg, and splinters from the bone kept poking at nerve endings. Making matters worse, his injured leg had been set poorly, and it ended up being two inches shorter than his other leg. Arnold walked with a terrible limp, grimacing with pain and embarrassed by his condition.

However, the physical pain from his injury was nothing compared to his emotional pain when he heard that Gates had received the honor of leading troops south. Ever since the win at Saratoga, Arnold had been very bitter over the fact that Gates had gotten all the glory and credit for the victory. Arnold's behavior in the battle, on the other hand, had not been admired. As a result, he had been placed in unimportant and unimpressive positions.

"Having become a cripple in the service of my country," Arnold once wrote angrily, "I little expected to meet [such] ungrateful returns."

Nonetheless, in the midst of all this pain and frustration, Benedict Arnold found time to fall in love and marry. Attempting to impress his new bride, Arnold rushed out and bought a huge house he couldn't afford. He was soon flat broke, and he began wondering how much the British might pay him to switch sides. He discussed this idea with his wife, Peggy Shippen. Peggy was a Loyalist who had all sorts of ties and connections to the British military. In fact, one of her best friends was John André, the British officer who had stayed in Benjamin Franklin's home and had stolen some of his possessions.

In no time at all, Arnold and André were sending letters back and forth, plotting and planning against the Americans. Then General Clinton, the new British commander, became involved. He enthusiastically encouraged Arnold, praising him and promising him a top general's position in the British army. Arnold was finally getting the credit and attention he had always believed he deserved. By the spring of 1780, Benedict Arnold was fully committed to becoming a traitor to his country. Then when Arnold was assigned the command of West Point, an American fort on the Hudson River in New York, Arnold and André came up with a plan that could do some serious damage to the Americans.

The command of West Point was actually a very impressive assignment. George Washington had always believed in Arnold, regardless of what others said about him. So when it was time to pick a new commander, Washington chose Arnold. Even though Arnold could be a bit extreme at times, Washington was certain he was dedicated to America and the fight for independence.

However, all Benedict Arnold was dedicated to in the summer of 1780 was his and André's devious plan. It would work like this: On a chosen day, the British would storm West Point. Arnold would intentionally misdirect his soldiers, giving bad orders and putting them in harm's way. The takeover of the fort by the British, then, would be simple. And there was going to be a bonus: Arnold would be sure to invite George Washington to West Point for an inspection on the same day as the attack. If everything went as planned, both West Point and George Washington would be captured by the British. General Clinton promised Arnold that he would receive a huge sum of money if everything went as planned.

It's frightening to think how close this plan came to succeeding. At the last minute, though, André was captured. He was returning from a late-night meeting with Arnold, traveling through some dark woods that were known to be full of thieves and spies. Suddenly, André was grabbed, and a knife was put to his throat.

"Where is your money?" the thieves demanded.

"Gentlemen, I have none about me," André replied.

The thieves didn't believe André, so they proceeded to yank at his clothing in search of money, pulling off his hat and boots. Tucked deep in the toe of one of André's boots were all the plans for the attack the very next day. At first, the thieves threw the papers down in disgust, but then one picked them up and began reading. Although the men were thieves, they were also Patriots. They rushed both André and the plans to the Continental Army's headquarters.

George Washington would later write that nothing in his entire life had upset him as much as finding out that Benedict Arnold was a traitor. His hands shook as he held the plans. He immediately recognized Arnold's handwriting, and tears came to his eyes. He looked around the room at his officers and then stared back at the plans.

"Arnold has betrayed me," he said in quiet voice. "Whom can we trust now?"

André was sentenced to death by hanging, but Benedict Arnold escaped. A spy had rushed to Arnold's house to warn him, even as Washington was crossing the river to confront him. Arnold jumped into a boat and took off as fast as he could row downriver to New York City, where he was protected by the British military. Eventually, Arnold would settle in London, but he slowly came to regret his betrayal. He was plagued by nightmares and depression. In America, he was referred to as "the old devil," and in England, he was treated with coldness and scorn. As it turned out, nobody on either side liked a traitor.

General Clinton was eager to get the British engaged in battle with the Southern states. He had grown so bored in New York City, waiting for some kind of action, that he and his officers had invented a fairly pathetic game called "fox hunting." In this game, a soldier on horseback would race through the streets trailing a bone on a rope behind him. A pack of five or six hounds would chase after the bone while Clinton and his staff galloped after them shouting "Tally ho!" and "Catch the fox!" Sometimes, to make things a little more interesting, bets were placed on which dog would get the bone.

"The winter of 1779 seems unusually long, and there is fearfully little to do," one British soldier in New York City wrote bluntly in his journal.

Finally, spring arrived. General Clinton had never really gotten over losing to General Moultrie in South Carolina back in 1776. It had been an embarrassing defeat, and now Clinton was determined to capture Charleston. Clinton had often regretted not having had a larger army in 1776. As a result, nearly 100 ships and 9,000 soldiers sailed out of New York City in April of 1780. This time, the harbor forts on the small islands guarding Charleston were useless, as the mighty British fleet blasted right through them. The British surrounded Charleston, and though the American soldiers fought bravely, they were outnumbered nearly two to one. Charleston fell into British control by May.

After capturing Charleston, General Clinton had satisfied his personal reasons for wanting to fight in the South. As a result, he returned to New York, turning over command of Charleston to a forty-two-year-old general named Charles Cornwallis. Cornwallis believed that terrorizing Southern Patriots was the way to break them down and destroy any dreams of victory they might have. In particular, "Cornwallis's raiders," as they were called, targeted plantations. They tore in on horseback, screaming loudly and setting fire to the fields and barns. Then they charged into plantation homes, stealing whatever they could grab and destroying everything else.

"The horses of the inhuman British seemed to tear up the earth," wrote Eliza Wilkinson, the wife of a plantation owner in South Carolina. "And the riders were bellowing out the most horrid curses imaginable . . . which chilled my whole frame."

However, not everyone dreaded the arrival of Cornwallis's raiders. Slaves had been promised freedom if they served in the British army. Since the summer of 1776, the British had used the fact that Americans enslaved other human beings as a way to mock the Declaration of Independence.

"They claim to demand freedom for all," laughed a member of Parliament, "while, at the very same time, they keep men in chains."

It was a sad fact that both the spirit of the Revolution and the Declaration of Independence were shamefully contradicted by the long history of slavery in America. In the mid-1700s, nearly half a million African Americans were owned as property. They had no rights, no freedoms, and certainly no independence.

"Slavery is a source of serious evils," Benjamin Franklin once wrote.

"I have opposed slavery my entire life," John Adams explained. "It is a foul contagion in the human character and an evil of colossal magnitude."

Although many Americans agreed with Franklin and Adams, many of the other Founding Fathers owned slaves. It would be nearly 100 years until slavery would be abolished in the United States. So, for the time being, slaves were willing to possibly lose their lives in an attempt to gain their freedom. In order to join the British army, a slave was required to run away from his master. Such an escape attempt could cost a slave his life. The British had no interest in rescuing slaves from plantations and liberating them. In fact, slaves taken during plantation raids were treated like stolen property: They were sold for a profit. Still, many thousands of slaves escaped and enlisted with British regiments.

Few African Americans were given the opportunity to actually fight as soldiers. Most of them performed the same jobs in the army that they had worked as slaves: digging ditches and roads, cooking, cleaning, and taking care of the horses. A few, however, served as spies and guides. Slaves knew the back roads and hidden trails through Southern swamps better than most people did. One slave, Quamino Dolly, guided British troops to Savannah, Georgia, along an unknown trail that led right up behind American troops. Thanks to Dolly's guidance, the surprised Americans were easily overtaken, and the British captured Savannah, a very important port city.

On the Patriots' side, several hundred free blacks, mainly in Philadelphia and New York, had joined the Continental Army. They were not allowed to serve when armies headed south, however.

"We fear it will set a bad example for the slaves," American officers claimed somewhat sheepishly. In other words, they worried that the sight of free black men might encourage even more slaves to run away and join the British army.

The Patriots, however, probably wished they had allowed the black soldiers to serve. Outnumbered and overpowered, the Americans lost battle after battle in the South. Making matters worse, Loyalists from New York and Pennsylvania headed south, hoping to encourage other Loyalists in the Southern states to join them.

Leading this large band of Loyalists was

a fierce twenty-six-year-old named Banastre Tarleton. Tarleton was what was known as a "dandy," meaning that he loved to dress in fancy clothing. Beneath the bright red velvet coats and the feathers in his fur hats, however, was the soul of a terribly brutal fighter.

As a group of American soldiers from Virginia headed south toward Charleston, they ran right into Tarleton and his men, known as "the Loyal Legion," on the North Carolina border. As a vicious battle began, the Americans realized they could not overpower the Legion. A Patriot carrying a white flag of surrender walked forward as the other Patriot soldiers laid their guns on the ground and raised their arms above their heads. What happened next was one of the most gruesome incidents of the American Revolution.

"No mercy! No quarter!" screamed Tarleton (*quarter* was a word that meant the same thing as *mercy*). Perhaps Tarleton was angry because his favorite horse had just been killed in the battle. Perhaps he simply saw an easy way to get rid of a bunch of Americans. Either way, what he did next was unforgivable. Waving his men onward, Tarleton and the Loyal Legion proceeded to slaughter the unarmed Americans with hatchets and knives, sparing no one. Nearly 150 Americans were hacked to pieces, while another 150 were cruelly left to die of their injuries on the battlefield.

Word of this horrible massacre spread quickly throughout the South.

"Revenge Banastre the Butcher!" came the angry shouts. "No mercy for the British!"

Now, thousands of Southerners, even those who had previously supported the British, rallied to fight for American freedom. Tarleton had hoped to drive fear into the minds of Southerners, but he had managed only to inspire hatred in their hearts.

About this time, General Horatio Gates and his army finally arrived in South Carolina. Everyone was expecting great things from Gates after his victory at Saratoga, but nearly everything went wrong for him in his first battle at Camden, South Carolina. To begin with, Gates's men were ragged and hungry after the long march south. Thinking it would give them strength, Gates ordered each of the soldiers to drink a pint of water mixed with molasses. This "medicine" afflicted every soldier with severe cramps and diarrhea.

Although the Patriot soldiers staggered into battle the next morning, Gates was still confident that they could overpower the smaller British army. Then he saw Banastre the Butcher and his Loyal Legion storming to the front lines to make way for Cornwallis and his Redcoats. Gates panicked. Perhaps he still could have rallied his soldiers to a victory, but he didn't even try. Instead, he turned around and began running and pushing soldiers out of his way. Gates then jumped onto a horse and took off at top speed, riding 170 miles in three days. Upon returning home, he was immediately removed from his position, publicly shamed, and never placed in command of an army again.

Then a new American commander, Nathanael Greene, took over in the South. George Washington was so fond of Greene that he referred to him as "Brother Nat." Although Washington still had not recovered from the sting of Arnold's betrayal, he felt that, of all his generals, Greene was the most trustworthy. And Greene so admired Washington that he decided to use one of Washington's tried and true battle tactics. Forcing the enemy to chase the Continental Army in the North had finally frustrated the British into giving up. Why not try that same approach in the South?

And so, for the remainder of 1780, Greene and his army lured the British into a chase through the Carolinas and Georgia, even going in circles at times. This chase generally resulted in small battles that Greene lost, but he kept on moving. Bit by bit he was wearing down Cornwallis's army and testing Cornwallis's patience. And, like Washington, Greene was blunt and completely unashamed about what he was doing.

"We fight, get beat, rise, and fight again," Greene said.

CHAPTER 12

"I have not yet begun to fight!"

"*W*ill this war never end?"

In England, more and more people were impatiently asking that question. This was a war King George had assured everyone would last only a few months, but now it was entering its sixth year. And because it had now expanded into a war with both France and Spain, it had become a terribly expensive war. Many British people, including some members of Parliament, began calling for an end to the war in America. It was costing more than it was worth. Clearly, Americans were absolutely determined to gain their independence. Why not just let them have it?

King George would not even consider it.

"I am determined never to acknowledge the independence of the Americans!" he shouted, adding that he fully intended to keep the American people harassed, poor, and frightened until they gave in. King George didn't care if this war lasted forever—he would not be pushed around by these rebels.

Because all the fighting was taking place thousands of miles away, across the Atlantic Ocean, it was perhaps easier for King George to brashly claim that the Americans would not push him around. However, in the fall of 1779, a young Patriot sea captain named John Paul Jones took the fight right to England's shores. His battle cemented many British people's belief that the Americans would never stop fighting, no matter how long the war went on.

At the beginning of the Revolution, America had had no navy at all. The Second Continental Congress had ordered a dozen warships to be built, but as soon as these ships set sail, they were destroyed or captured by the British. England had the largest and strongest navy on earth, and many British soldiers thought it was foolish for the Americans to even consider fighting against it. The navies were so unevenly matched that even some Patriots admitted that the contest seemed ridiculous.

However, John Paul Jones wasn't laughing. He had faith in the small, struggling navy, and he believed that even if the Americans could not overpower the British on the sea, they could at least compete and begin to gain respect. Physically, Jones seemed like an unlikely naval hero-to-be. He was barely five feet, five inches tall and quite thin, with a face that was often described as "girlish."

"His voice is soft and still and small," John Adams wrote after meeting Jones, "but his eyes have keenness and wildness in them."

There was indeed a wildness about John Paul Jones. He had a ferocious temper that had become greatly feared, even among his own sailors. Jones had killed two sailors in his command after he had had disagreements with them. But even more ferocious than his temper was John Paul Jones's desire to prove himself in battle. He would get the chance in September of 1779.

Because of Jones's reputation as a fierce fighter and successful captain, the French decided to give him command of a six-ship squadron of old merchant ships. These were sailing vessels that had originally been designed to carry cargo, not to go into battle. But that didn't bother Jones. He had the ships outfitted with cannons and guns, gathered the bravest sailors he knew, and headed directly toward the British coast. His goal was to damage as many port towns in England as possible, and if that meant a battle at sea with British warships, Jones was ready for it.

On the evening of September 23, 1779, John Paul Jones was aboard his ship the *Bonhomme Richard*, named after Benjamin Franklin's publication, *Poor Richard's Almanac*. Just as the sun was beginning to set, Jones led his other five ships into British territory. In order to confuse, or possibly fool, the British, Jones's ships were flying the British flag. Now, as Jones turned a corner around a cliff, he and his ships ran smack into forty-one British supply ships being escorted by two warships, the *Countess of Scarborough* and the *Serapis*.

Jones thought he had hit the jackpot. If his six ships could bring down the two British warships, forty-one ships packed with supplies would be his. However, when the *Scarborough* and the *Serapis* sailed over to investigate, all of Jones's other ships took off. The *Scarborough* followed them, and Jones found himself alone. It looked as if there was going to be a showdown between the *Bonhomme Richard* and the *Serapis*.

"What ship is that?" came the voice of the captain of the *Serapis*.

"Come a little closer and I will tell you," shouted Jones.

As the *Serapis* sailed closer, the captain mistook Jones's ship for a mere merchant vessel. "What are you carrying?" he called to Jones in a relieved voice.

Now there was a long pause. The moon had risen, and it was shining on the flagpole of the *Bonhomme Richard*. At the very same moment that Jones responded with "Bullets and shot!" a twenty-five-foot-long American flag replaced the British flag and fluttered proudly in the sea breeze.

Instantly, the guns and cannons on each ship boomed in a volley of fire. But the biggest cannons on the *Bonhomme Richard* were poor, second-hand weapons, and within minutes, two of those big cannons blew up. The explosion killed half of Jones's crew and left the surviving sailors only small guns with which to defend their ship. The British captain saw his advantage.

"Do you surrender?" shouted the captain.

Above the noise of the battle and the cries of the wounded and dying came John Paul Jones's famous reply, a response that would become the motto of the United States Navy: "I have not yet begun to fight!"

And Jones meant what he said. Not having the gun power to defeat the *Serapis*, he slammed his boat directly into the British warship and began throwing ladders onto its deck.

"Come on, lads!" he shouted to his men. "We've got her now!"

The remaining American sailors swarmed the *Serapis*, confusing and terrifying its crew. Handfuls of grenades were tossed into the ship's ammunition stores, creating terrible explosions and fires.

"The dead were lying in heaps," one sailor later wrote. "Blood and brains and entrails reached over one's shoes."

Finally, the British surrendered—and just in the nick of time. Even as Jones was tying up the surviving British sailors to take them prisoner, the *Bonhomme Richard*, full of holes from cannon shots, sank to the bottom of the North Sea. The next morning, however, Jones took command of the *Serapis* instead and sailed his prisoners to France.

That victory made John Paul Jones one of the biggest superstars of the American Revolution. Poetry was written in his honor, and songs of his amazing battle were sung in taverns and meeting halls throughout America. Artists rushed to paint his portrait, and everyone wanted to see this ferocious little sea captain. Nonetheless, the defeat of one warship barely reduced the overall power of the British navy. The damage it *did* do, however, was perhaps worse.

"*Not yet begun to fight*, we must begin to fear, is the sentiment of every American Patriot," one London newspaper reported. "This war shall never end, for, truly, the Americans will not allow it."

And back in the American South, there was certainly no indication that the British were going to win any time soon. General Cornwallis was still chasing after Nathanael Greene, who had become amazingly skilled at leading the British on a wild-goose chase.

"We are like a crab," Greene once joked about his army. "We can run in any direction as long as it's away."

Cornwallis, however, was not amused by this joke. His army was getting worn down; supplies were running out; and nothing was being accomplished. Cornwallis was winning battle after battle, but this was only because the Americans kept retreating and moving on. It was beginning to occur to Cornwallis that the British would never be able to deliver a knockout punch in the South unless they could completely surround the Americans and capture them in a surprise attack.

This was not likely to happen for a number of reasons.

Word had rapidly spread of Tarleton and his massacre of the defenseless Americans who had surrendered near the Virginia border. From parts of Virginia, North Carolina, and what would later become Kentucky and Tennessee, bands of angry Patriot frontiersmen hurried to confront the British in South Carolina. Because these men had to cross both the Appalachian and Blue Ridge mountains to get to their destination, they became known as "the Overmountain Men."

Numbering more than 1,000, the Overmountain Men marched for days. They dressed in fringed leather hunting shirts and coonskin caps, and every man carried a long rifle and long knives.

"Revenge Tarleton! Revenge Tarleton!" they chanted as they marched.

Cornwallis and his second-in-command, Major Patrick Ferguson, were not particularly worried when they received word that the Overmountain Men were heading their way.

"We have no intention of running from them," Ferguson scoffed. "They are nothing more than a loud rabble."

When Cornwallis and Ferguson reached Kings Mountain, South Carolina, they decided to wait for the Overmountain Men there. Covered with huge boulders, Kings Mountain was a natural fortress as well as a high lookout.

"God Almighty and all the rebels out of Hell could not beat us here!" Ferguson brashly claimed.

But within twenty-four hours, the British army had been soundly defeated, and Major Ferguson lay dead on the mountainside. The Overmountain Men had surprised the British, arriving much sooner than expected and surrounding the British on all sides. This, combined with the sharpshooting skills of the frontiersmen, proved to be too much for the British. And when Ferguson was killed,

Cornwallis reluctantly ordered a retreat.

Although Cornwallis's frustration was mounting steadily, he pushed on. After all, the Americans had won only a few battles in the South. Surely they would begin to weaken soon. But as Cornwallis's army continued its pursuit of Greene's men, things got worse. The Redcoats were constantly ambushed by roving bands of "guerrillas"—unofficial soldiers who used unusual methods, such as surprise attacks and destruction of property. Although *guerrilla* is a Spanish word meaning "little war," these little wars would ultimately drive the British out of the South. Guerrilla fighters traveled in groups of 100 or fewer men, and they launched their surprise attacks from trees, from behind rocks, and even from rooftops. Then, as quickly as they had appeared, the guerrillas would vanish into the woods or the surrounding swamps.

These guerrillas were led by men who knew all the secret trails and hiding places. The most famous of these leaders was a South Carolinian named Francis Marion. Although Marion had been born one month early and had been so small and frail as an infant that he had been able to fit into a one-quart drinking mug, he had grown into a strong, quiet young man. Marion had spent many hours exploring the swamps near his home. He had befriended Native Americans who had taught him how to survive in the wilderness—and how to surprise an enemy.

By 1780, Francis Marion had become the most-feared of the guerrilla leaders. He led his band of men on marches through the swamps in the middle of the night, barely making a sound. If the band's horses had to cross a bridge near the enemy, pine straw and blankets were laid across the bridge to muffle the noise. It was rumored that Marion and his men never rested in the same place twice.

Both Cornwallis and Tarleton found themselves constantly shot at and terrorized by Marion and his guerrillas. Time after time, these two British generals tried to chase Francis Marion through the swamps, but they managed only to get lost, mosquito-bitten, and exhausted.

"That damned old fox!" complained Tarleton after losing Marion's trail for the last time. "Even the Devil himself could not catch him!"

And so Francis Marion's famous nickname was born: "the Swamp Fox."

By the spring of 1781, General Cornwallis had had enough. He had spent a year running all over the South, accomplishing very little other than losing men and being made to look like a fool. Now he began thinking about Virginia. His time in the South had taught him that the Carolinas and Georgia could not survive without the help and supplies they received from ports in Virginia. If Virginia could be taken by the British, the entire South would collapse.

British troops were already stationed in Virginia—in towns near Chesapeake Bay, where their fleets of warships were docked. Cornwallis believed that if he and his men came up from the South while the British commander, General Clinton, and his men came down from New York City, the Patriots would be entirely outnumbered and overwhelmed. They believed that this time there would be no way for the Americans to win or escape.

"I am quite tired of marching all about the South," Cornwallis wrote to Clinton in April of 1781. "If we mean an offensive war in America, we must bring our whole force into Virginia."

Clinton disagreed. In fact, Clinton disagreed with nearly everything Cornwallis said or did. The two men had completely opposite approaches to the war. Clinton liked to take his time, sit back and analyze the situation, and move cautiously into battle. Cornwallis, on the other hand, didn't like to analyze. He preferred to jump right into the fighting. Although Clinton was head of the British armed forces, Cornwallis regularly disregarded orders from him. And when Cornwallis ignored Clinton altogether and began writing to King George for orders, Clinton blew up.

"I can never be cordial with such a man," Clinton claimed. "He is completely incompetent."

Now Clinton instructed Cornwallis to return north. Clinton was nearly certain that Washington was planning an attack on the British in New York, and he wanted to have as many troops as possible prepared for that battle. Clinton knew that French reinforcements were on the way to help the Americans. Where and when the French were going to land, Clinton wasn't sure, but he was willing to bet that it was going to be New York City—and soon.

However, as usual, Cornwallis did as he pleased. He disregarded Clinton's order and began marching his army to Virginia. George Washington received the news of Cornwallis's move and was quite worried. What was going on? Washington had neither the manpower nor the supplies to fight battles in both New York and Virginia. The Continental Army, still camped outside New York City, had dwindled to barely 3,500 struggling men. It was in its worst shape ever.

"The American army was composed of men of every age, even children," one observer wrote that spring. "They were almost naked, unpaid, and rather poorly fed."

The British army, on the other hand, was well fed and brightly uniformed—and had about twice as many troops in New York as the Americans had. As Cornwallis's troops marched toward Virginia, Washington paced and fretted. He knew that nothing short of a miracle could save the Americans this time.

"We are at the end of our tether," Washington wrote in desperation, "and now or never our deliverance must come."

CHAPTER 13

"The world turned upside down"

"The moment I heard of America, I loved her. The moment I knew she was fighting for freedom, I burned with a desire of bleeding for her!"

These were the passionate words of the young French leader, the Marquis de Lafayette. Lafayette's parents had died, leaving him an orphan—with a huge inheritance—when he was only 13. Without parents, Lafayette had learned to take on adult responsibilities at a young age. In fact, when he was barely 19, he had decided to sail to America in order to fight in the Revolution. Although he spoke almost no English, and had almost no military experience, he was determined.

Some American officers who met this energetic young man just rolled their eyes. They had seen plenty of "glory seekers"—would-be soldiers from Europe who were more interested in becoming famous than in helping America. But the Marquis de Lafayette was different, and George Washington recognized that at once. Washington made the young Frenchman an honorary major general, and spent a great deal of time working with him. Thanks to Washington's guidance, Lafayette soon became fluent in English and became a wise, decisive, brave officer.

In time, Washington and Lafayette became best friends. Although it seems an unlikely friendship, Lafayette had never really known a father, and Washington had never had a son. Their relationship filled those voids. Washington often told Lafayette to think of him as "friend and father." And Lafayette named his first son "George Washington Lafayette," once joking with Washington that he was glad his son had Washington's name and not his looks. Washington, who was not particularly well-known for a sense of humor, reportedly laughed aloud and said, "So true, my dear Lafayette."

Now, in a time of crisis, Washington turned to Lafayette. As soon as Cornwallis reached Virginia, he began attacking towns, destroying farms, and generally terrorizing Virginians. Outfitting Lafayette with a small army, Washington sent him to Virginia, hoping that he could at least stall Cornwallis's rampage. This was not to be.

"I am not afraid of this boy general," Cornwallis sneered. His army far outnumbered Lafayette's, and his wild and random attacks were nearly impossible to predict or prevent.

"Lord Cornwallis's abilities are more alarming to me than his superiority of forces," Lafayette admitted in a letter to Washington. "To speak plain English, I am devilish afraid of him."

For much of the summer, Cornwallis and his troops traveled about destroying as much of Virginia as they could. They set Petersburg on fire and shot cannons at Richmond. They destroyed the state's new capitol building in Charlottesville and sent the dreaded Banastre Tarleton out to taunt and scare people in the countryside. Back in New York, General Clinton was still fuming over the fact that Cornwallis had defiantly ignored his order to return to New York City.

"My wonder at this move of Lord Cornwallis will never cease," the general said angrily. Then he added, "Still, he has made it, and we must make the best of it."

Since autumn was approaching, General Clinton insisted that Cornwallis find some place in Virginia to build a camp and settle for the winter. Only because he knew he would need protection from the weather, Cornwallis agreed.

Encouraged by this, Clinton then insisted that Cornwallis send at least half of his troops back to New York. Clinton felt he needed those troops in order to be prepared for the attack he still believed was coming from the Americans and the French. Cornwallis didn't even bother to respond to this demand, deciding he would keep all 9,000 men for himself.

Cornwallis chose the small farming town of Yorktown, near Chesapeake Bay, as the site for his winter camp. Years earlier, Yorktown had been an important port for tobacco trade, but now the sleepy little town was nearly deserted. This suited Cornwallis just fine. Suiting him even more, however, was the very deep York River that ran past Yorktown. It would be perfect for shipping in supplies and, Cornwallis hoped, more soldiers—once Clinton realized that capturing Virginia was the way to go.

Since Lafayette had been unable to stop Cornwallis, he decided to spy on him instead. When Lafayette sent a letter to Washington explaining that Cornwallis and his troops had settled in Yorktown, near the mouth of Chesapeake Bay, Washington was alarmed. The British already had control of both the New York City and Charleston harbors. If they gained power over Chesapeake Bay as well, the British would control shipping for nearly all of America.

For some time, Washington had been focused on attacking Clinton in New York. But he couldn't do that until more French soldiers arrived to help him. Now the British were on the verge of taking over another important port, and there was nothing Washington could do to stop them. By early August of 1781, George Washington was desperate. It was at this very point that the "deliverance" Washington had hoped for finally arrived.

On August 14, a message arrived: "Admiral Count de Grasse can assist you. He is en route to the Chesapeake from the West Indies with twenty-eight warships and 3,000 troops."

Suddenly, everything changed. Looking at a map, Washington ran one finger down from New York and another one up from the West Indies, a large group of islands in the Caribbean. If everything was timed just perfectly, Cornwallis's army could be trapped—squeezed between Washington's army and the French Admiral de Grasse's troops. And if Cornwallis's army were forced to surrender, it would be a blow so severe that the British would not be able to recover from it. It would almost certainly mean victory for the Americans.

Washington barely slept for the next five days. He worked nonstop to get everything ready for his troops to travel to Yorktown. Joining the Continental Army would be 6,000 French troops that had been camped in Rhode Island for nearly a year, waiting for a battle. Leading these French soldiers was Jean-Baptiste Rochambeau. Rochambeau was a French commander who spoke only a few words of English. However, he knew just how to inspire soldiers—both French and American—when it was time to fight.

Less than a week after Washington received the message about Count de Grasse, nearly 9,000 soldiers had been organized to travel to Virginia from New York. However, none of the soldiers knew exactly where they were headed. For once during the Revolution, a secret had been kept completely under wraps. Some soldiers placed bets on where they were going, while others worried that even Washington didn't know. Some whispered that George Washington had finally lost his mind.

Washington loved it.

"If one cannot deceive his own soldiers," Washington wrote, "he has no hope of deceiving the enemy."

And fooling the enemy was critical. The French and American soldiers would have to march within twenty-four miles of Clinton's Redcoats in Manhattan. Washington did everything he could think of to fool Clinton. He sent fake letters discussing an upcoming attack on New York City, knowing that the letters would be intercepted by British spies. He sent small regiments of soldiers to Staten Island to set up tents and survey the land so that the British would think Washington was planning to launch his attack from there. Washington even had those soldiers build large bread-baking ovens to make it appear as though the American troops would be stationed on Staten Island for a long time.

And on August 19, 1781, the French and American forces marched almost right under the nose of General Clinton. But he did nothing. Many felt that there was no way Clinton could have been totally unaware of what was happening.

"Any enemy of any boldness or skill would have seized an opportunity so favorable to him and so embarrassing to us," one of the French officers wrote. "I do not understand General Clinton's indifference."

But it was this exact lack of action that Washington had been hoping for. Any interference with his troops' movement would have been extremely costly. Once past Manhattan, the French and American soldiers began moving very quickly. It was now a race against the clock. De Grasse had told Washington that he could remain in Chesapeake Bay for only a very short time. What if de Grasse got there before Washington did? Would he turn around and leave? Worse yet, what if de Grasse was late?

Washington had instructed Lafayette to secretly surround Cornwallis's camp in Yorktown to keep the Redcoats from escaping. However, Washington knew that if Cornwallis was determined to escape, his army could clearly overpower Lafayette's. In other words, the secret must remain safe. Cornwallis must continue to believe that the Continental Army had no intention of moving into Virginia.

In Manhattan, General Clinton continued to be fooled. He was so convinced that Washington was planning to attack Manhattan that he became overwhelmed with worry and confusion. Somehow, he had convinced himself that the Continental Army outnumbered the British when, actually, the opposite was true. His spies rushed to tell him that they had witnessed Washington's troops moving south, but Clinton refused to believe it.

"The Chesapeake is the object!" one spy frantically warned Clinton. "Everything is in motion. You must act!"

And yet Clinton remained in New York, still keeping an eye out for Washington who, by this time, was well on his way to the Chesapeake. Not until one of de Grasse's ships was actually sighted heading north toward Virginia did Clinton finally realize his mistake. In a panic, he sent Cornwallis a message warning him. Then he wrote to King George:

"Things appear to be coming fast to a crisis. . . . I will exert myself to the utmost to save Lord Cornwallis."

Clinton may not have been concerned about Cornwallis; however, he *was* concerned about his own reputation. He did not want his lack of response to be the reason for Britain losing the war. In a flurry of action, Clinton gathered soldiers and warships, and took off toward the Chesapeake at top speed. Washington and de Grasse were already far ahead of him, however. In this all-out race to Yorktown, it began to look as though Clinton would not have a chance to help Cornwallis; he had simply waited too long to act.

Washington, however, was still very cautious and quite worried. Weeks had passed since anyone had actually heard from de Grasse. If something had happened to him, the entire plan for attacking Yorktown would fail.

"I am distressed beyond expression to know what has become of the Count de Grasse," Washington wrote to Lafayette. "If you hear anything new, send it. I am almost all impatience and anxiety."

Finally, on September 5, 1781, word reached Washington that de Grasse's ships had indeed reached the Chesapeake. In fact, they had just defeated the British warships there. George Washington had always maintained the reputation of being a very serious man who rarely showed much emotion publicly, but when he received that news, Washington could not contain his excitement.

"It was a most amazing sight," wrote a French officer. "A tall officer in blue was jumping up and down shouting, 'de Grasse! de Grasse!' He was waving in one hand a hat and in the other a white handkerchief. The dancing figure seemed to be His Excellency General Washington, but, of course, that was impossible."

The figure was indeed Washington, however. This was, without a doubt, the most exciting news Washington had received during the entire Revolutionary War. De Grasse's victory meant that additional British ships—and soldiers and supplies—would be unable to reach Virginia from the Chesapeake Bay. And now, when all of the French and American troops arrived from the north, there would be no escape for Cornwallis. More than half of all the British soldiers in America were camped at Yorktown. If they were captured or forced to surrender, Washington knew that it would mean American victory.

Washington was so relieved and encouraged by this turn of events that he decided to briefly visit his home, Mount Vernon. The march to Yorktown passed very close to Washington's beloved farm, and it had been six years since he had seen it. Washington's wife, Martha, had visited him often at the winter camps, but Washington had never been able to find the time to visit Martha in their own home. Washington had desperately missed Mount Vernon. Now, as he walked through the front door, his servants stared at him in shock.

"It hurt to look upon a face so changed by the storms of campaigns and the mighty cares which had burdened his mind during more than six years of absence," one servant would later comment.

The war had certainly taken its toll on its greatest leader, but now, perhaps, the storms and burdens would be coming to an end. Farther south, in Yorktown, Cornwallis was beginning to realize that the British could not win the war. De Grasse had beaten back the British ships, and even as Cornwallis was making final desperate preparations, Clinton was shamefully sailing back to New York. American and French troops now surrounded Cornwallis. No food, supplies, or help could get in, and no British soldiers could escape.

Cornwallis, however, was stubborn. He decided to put all his soldiers' energy into reinforcing the British forts. The British would remain in Yorktown as long as they could. Cornwallis believed that if he could hold off the Americans long enough, Clinton would surely return with more men and more ships. But weeks passed, and no help arrived. Making matters worse, the Americans had now begun bombarding the British, firing cannonballs into their camp around the clock. Once, as Cornwallis nervously watched the bombardment, a messenger standing next to him had his head completely ripped off by a cannonball.

"We are desperate!" Cornwallis wrote to Clinton. "You must come quickly."

When the days dragged on and no word arrived from Clinton, Cornwallis made a horrifying decision. Provisions for the soldiers had nearly run out, and some men were already beginning to grow weak and sick from hunger. Cornwallis decided that he could no longer afford to feed the former slaves, who had risked their lives to join the British forces. In fact, he no longer wanted them inside the British camp at all. Instead of receiving freedom, as they had been promised, African Americans were forced to walk directly into the Patriots' gunfire.

By mid-October of 1781, the British soldiers often saw Cornwallis sitting in his tent with his head in his hands. In a last-ditch effort, he had tried to sneak his army across the York River in a midnight escape, but the soldiers had been forced back almost immediately. Waiting in the bay were all of de Grasse's warships, with their huge cannons and guns pointed directly at the British. Washington was now on the verge of using those French warships to utterly destroy Cornwallis's army. Cornwallis finally made a bitter decision on the morning of October 17.

In the haze of the smoke from the cannons and gunfire, a small British soldier in a bright red coat began walking directly toward the enemy. He played a steady drumroll, his legs shaking as he walked. As he drew closer, the Americans could see that he was just a child—a British drummer boy.

"Hold your fire! Hold your fire!" came the excited shouts of the ragged American soldiers.

Then, just behind the boy, came a British officer. The Americans could barely believe their eyes. Above his head the officer waved a flag—the white flag of surrender.

The world had been turned upside down.

CHAPTER 14

"A people who defy kings"

*"O*h God, it is all over!"

When England's prime minister, Frederick North, learned of the defeat of the British at Yorktown, he paced back and forth in Parliament, crying out these words again and again. It had been North who, sixteen years earlier, had confidently told the very young King George that "America must fear you before she can love you." In the end, America had never backed down in fear, and any love it had ever had for King George was long gone.

King George responded to the defeat as though it hadn't really happened. He refused to admit that America had crushed the British.

"Yorktown does not cause the slightest alteration in those principles of my conduct which have directed me in past time," the king stubbornly announced. King George was saying, in other words, that losing at Yorktown meant nothing, that he was not going to change his mind about America's independence. In fact, the king now called for the British army to be doubled in America. He demanded that the war effort continue at an even higher level of intensity.

The British people, however, said enough was enough. Although they were reluctant to speak out against their king, this was getting ridiculous. The cost of the seemingly endless war was pushing Britain toward bankruptcy, and many people had become both jobless and homeless. In addition, during the course of the war, many British people had grown to both admire the Americans and sympathize with them.

"It is like the David and Goliath story," one British newspaper had said of the Revolution after it had dragged on for years. "One wants to see David conquer."

King George went into a rage. He threatened to give up the throne if the British people didn't support the war. The British people didn't really care. More important, the British Parliament agreed with the people, and passed a resolution calling it treason for anyone to even suggest that the war should continue. And the dreaded punishment for treason had not changed a bit over the years. The thought of being hanged, cut open, set on fire, and chopped into four pieces put an abrupt end to the king's stubbornness. Reluctantly, King George III began accepting the fact that the Americans were free. The thirteen colonies would never again belong to England.

Back in America, General Clinton had finally gotten around to taking troops and warships to the Chesapeake to help Cornwallis. The only problem was that he arrived about a week after the British had surrendered! When news of this huge mistake reached England, Clinton's reputation was ruined. He was removed from his position in disgrace. Although General Clinton was not the only British leader to make mistakes during the American Revolution, he is often held responsible for England's loss. On the other hand, Cornwallis was regarded as something of a hero—a brave general who had fought to the bitter end with no help from his commanding officer. He would go on to have a long and honored military career.

Word of England's surrender spread rapidly throughout America. Like the British soldiers, many Americans simply could not believe that their young army had actually defeated the greatest military power on earth. In Philadelphia, where people had been able to follow the war more closely, the celebration was instant. Fireworks filled the air, and the streets overflowed with people shouting, ringing bells, drinking, and dancing. Bands paraded all night playing "Yankee Doodle," a song that had become the theme of the Revolution, even though the British had originally written it to mock the Patriots.

Thousands of people rushed to Yorktown to witness the official surrender ceremony, which took place on October 19, 1781. They all stood quietly on the hillsides as 8,000 British soldiers marched slowly down Williamsburg Road. Most of the soldiers were wearing new uniforms they had received only a few days earlier. They wore them to show their pride. However, the contrast between the immaculate British soldiers and the dirty, ragged Americans—most of whom had never even owned a uniform—only made their humiliation worse. Many of the British soldiers were crying and avoiding the eyes of the Americans. Others were drunk and glaring at them.

Finally, George Washington and Rochambeau, both on horseback, stopped in the middle of the field. Everyone waited in hushed anticipation. This was the greatest moment of glory for the victors—the moment when the commander of the British forces would hand over his sword to the commander of the American forces. However, the British commander, Cornwallis, had remained in camp, complaining of a headache. In his place, he had sent a major general, Charles O'Hara.

O'Hara rode over to Washington and Rochambeau, and stared at them in confusion. Finally, he offered the sword to Rochambeau, who smiled and shook his head.

"We are subordinate to the Americans," the French commander said quietly.

O'Hara turned red when he realized his error, quickly offering the sword to Washington instead.

Then, to everyone's astonishment, Washington, too, refused the sword. Washington was not the kind of man to be petty or small, but he considered it a deliberate insult for Cornwallis to be absent. It was even more insulting for him to have sent a much lower-ranking officer in his place. It had been a long, extremely hard-fought war, and Washington was not going to let this moment of honor for America be tarnished. Instead, he pointed to one of *his* major generals, Benjamin Lincoln. Finally, the sword was passed from O'Hara to Lincoln to signify surrender. It is believed, though there is much debate about this point, that Washington reached down from his horse and lightly touched the sword to make the surrender official.

Following this, each British soldier laid his gun onto the growing pile of weapons. Many of the soldiers grumbled and swore; some of them threw their guns so angrily that the weapons broke. In general, the British soldiers had always despised the French, and now they hated the Americans just as much. But not everyone who had fought on the British side felt that way. One Hessian soldier eyed the Americans with a good deal of respect.

"Out of this rabble," he said, looking across the wide field full of weary but victorious American soldiers, "has risen a people who defy kings."

Although the official surrender of the British took place in October of 1781, the Revolutionary War would not officially end until September of 1783. The British still occupied Charleston and other cities in the South; thousands of troops were still in New York City; and Loyalists and Patriots continued attacking one another in small skirmishes. It would take more than two years, but all of the British soldiers were finally sent back to England, and the South was eventually free of their presence. Loyalists, no longer having a king to remain loyal to, either left America or kept their opinions to themselves.

All that stood between the final separation of England and America was a signed treaty. But even this took a long time. For one thing, America had promised France that it would be included in the treaty process. This promise was not kept, however, causing France to grow suspicious of America. Next, the French began holding secret meetings with the British, discussing ways to keep the Americans from moving farther westward, across the frontier. Soon, accusations were flying. Tempers flared, and no one was willing to sit down and work out a treaty.

Finally, a peace agreement was reached, and the Treaty of Paris (so named because it was signed in Paris) officially ended the war. King George had changed his tune during the two years following the defeat at Yorktown. Now he claimed that he didn't really care about America anyway, and he was glad to be rid of those annoying thirteen colonies.

However, as he read the Treaty of Paris to the members of Parliament, he suddenly paused as he stumbled over a certain word. Appearing to be struggling with his emotions, King George tried to continue. His voice cracked, and a dark frown covered his face. Finally, however, he was able to utter the difficult word: *independence*.

Nine days after the last British soldiers left America in December of 1783, George Washington invited all of the officers who had served under him during the war to a special dinner at the Fraunces Tavern in New

York City. Washington was very tired. He was barely recognizable as the same man who had taken command of the untried and untrained Continental Army seven years earlier. Now all Washington wanted was to return to Mount Vernon.

"I am retiring within myself," he wrote to Lafayette. "I shall be able to view the solitary walk and tread the paths of life with heartfelt satisfaction. . . . I will move gently down the stream of life until I sleep with my fathers."

That is what he planned to tell his officers at the dinner. However, the words were not as easy to say aloud as they had been to write in a letter. When Washington entered the dining room and saw all his faithful and hard-working officers waiting for him, tears filled his eyes. He poured a glass of wine and looked around the silent room. Then, with a voice shaking with emotion, he said, "With a heart full of love and gratitude I now take leave of you. I most devoutly wish that your latter days may be as prosperous and happy as your former ones have been glorious and honorable."

Washington then asked each officer to come up and shake his hand in farewell. The first to come to Washington was his old friend General Knox. Knox was the cannon expert who had directed the transport of many tons of cannons from Fort Ticonderoga to Boston in the dead of winter in 1776. That had been a tough job, but it was not nearly as tough as saying goodbye to his beloved General Washington. Knox reached forward to shake hands, but then he changed his mind. Instead, he put both his arms around Washington and burst into tears. Suddenly, every man in the room was crying.

"Such a scene of sorrow and weeping I had never before witnessed," one officer later wrote. "The thought that we were about to part from the man who had conducted us through a long and bloody war, and under whose conduct the independence of our country had been achieved . . . that we should see his face no more in this world seemed to me utterly impossible."

Washington waved goodbye to his officers that evening, believing he'd never see them again. "I have had my day," he said quietly as he left the Fraunces Tavern.

Little did George Washington know that his "day" was far from over. In fact, Washington's "retirement" lasted only a few years. "The United States of America," as the country was now called, may have won its independence, but no one really had any idea about how to govern this new land. At first, some suggested that Washington should be crowned king. Washington, however, quickly pointed out that royal rule would go against everything Americans had just fought for.

As Thomas Paine had pointed out in *Common Sense*, ordinary people could govern a country.

After turning down the offer to be king, Washington attempted once again to disappear into retirement. But new troubles began drawing Washington back into the debate over what was best for the future of America.

"The Revolution is not over!" one writer claimed. "The American war is over, but this is far from being the case with the American Revolution."

Although the bloodshed of war had come to an end, the battle of ideas and words among disagreeing American people was just beginning. It was still difficult for people to think of the states as being truly united. The loyalty of many Americans was still to their own state—not to their new country. The same old fights over boundaries, taxes, and laws began flaring up. Making matters worse, the United States was flat broke after fighting a long, expensive war. And now there was no "mother country" to turn to for help.

Because there was no strong national government, states began making their own decisions about how to tax their citizens. Many of the taxes were so ridiculously high that no one could pay them. Still, state governments demanded the money, and before long, some states began threatening to take farms, land, and homes away from those who were unable to pay the outrageous taxes. Naturally, people rebelled. Small skirmishes broke out, and crowds shouted and protested in the streets.

In London, King George and Loyalists who had moved to England read the news of America's problems with glee.

"They will never be able to govern themselves!" they said happily. "It is only a matter of time before they come back asking us for help."

But that time never came. Although Washington was not eager to return to politics, he was not about to sit idly by and watch his country fall apart. Once again, Washington traveled to Philadelphia to meet with members of the new Congress of the Confederation. For many months, the nation's founders discussed how their national government should work. Out of their debates would finally come the official document that outlines how the federal government is organized: the United States Constitution.

Leading the federal government, Congress decided, would be a person known as the "president." On February 4, 1789, George Washington was unanimously chosen by Congress for this job. Many in Congress and beyond were not sure how to address Washington in his new role. Some continued to call him "Your Excellency," while others, even though they knew Washington was not a king, could not help calling him "Your Majesty."

"Please," the modest Washington finally said to those who stumbled over his title, "simply call me 'Mr. President.'"

The American victory in the Revolutionary War has often been called an unbelievable win against overwhelming odds—even a miracle. But was it? Calling the victory a "miracle" takes away from the undying dedication of the American people during those six years of suffering and, often, downright hopelessness.

"The Revolution was in the minds of the people," John Adams once wrote. A vision of freedom and independence burned like a bright light in the minds of colonists, and it never dimmed. From the first shots at Lexington all the way to the surrender at Yorktown, Americans embraced the belief that common people *could* defy kings. While the British had bigger and better armies, a real navy, and superior weapons, the Americans had something that, in the end, proved even stronger: Every Patriot carried a remarkable and inspiring idea of a new government and a new country.

"You cannot conquer an idea with an army," Thomas Paine would later explain.

And, indeed, it was the power of the idea of freedom and independence that ultimately carried the American people to victory.